Music through the Dark

Asian and Pacific American
Transcultural Studies

Russell C. Leong
General Editor

Music through the Dark

**A TALE OF
SURVIVAL IN
CAMBODIA**

Bree Lafreniere

*University
of Hawai'i
Press
Honolulu*

*in association
with UCLA
Asian American
Studies Center
Los Angeles*

Printed in the United States of America
05 04 03 02 01 00   5 4 3 2

Library of Congress Cataloging-in-
Publication Data
Lafreniere, Bree, 1959–
    Music through the dark : a tale of survival
in Cambodia / Bree Lafreniere.
        p. cm. — (Intersections)
    ISBN 0–8248–2227–7 (cloth : alk. paper)—
    ISBN 0–8248–2266–8 (paper : alk. paper)
    1. Kravanh, Daran, 1954– 2. Cambodia—
History 1953–1975 3. Cambodia—History 1975–
4. Political refugees—Cambodia—Biography.
5. Political refugees—United States—Biography. I. Kravanh, Daran, 1954– II. Title.
III. Intersections (Honolulu, Hawaii)
DS554.83.K73 L34   2000
959.604—dc21   99–053430

University of Hawai'i Press books are printed
on acid-free paper and meet the guidelines for
permanence and durability of the Council on
Library Resources.

Printed by The Maple-Vail Book
Manufacturing Group

This book is dedicated to my family who were not allowed to survive:
To my brilliant father, Kong By, and my loving mother, Chan Hoeun,
*   my brothers*
Chamroeun, Bunly, Sthany, Dararith, Samnang, and Rithy
*   and my sister Raksmey*
may your souls live forever in this book

And to my one living brother, Reatrey,
my two sons, Kiry and Chunneath,
and all my beloved Cambodian people
may this book honor you and remind you to love and keep peace always

—*Daran Kravanh*

Contents

Accordion *(ə-kor'di-ən), n. a keyed musical instrument with a bellows, which is pressed to force air through reeds, from the root word "Accord"*

Accord *(ə-kord') v.t. [L. ad, to + cor, heart] to cause to agree or harmonize 2. to grant, to give, to allow, to spare, to reconcile 3. to be in agreement, unity or harmony. n. 1. a settlement of conflicting opinions.*

A Note on the Storytelling Process

We began this story in 1992 while working together in the Refugee Assistance Program of Catholic Community Services in Tacoma, Washington. Although it is written in Daran's voice, it is not a translation, an oral history, or an autobiography. Rather it is a literary account of a personal experience told by one person and written by another with all the interpretations of such a transfer. It was produced by the interplay of opposites—objectivity and subjectivity, intimacy and distance, male and female, Cambodian and American, Buddhist and Christian. Over the four years of conversations, we never used a tape recorder. Instead, Bree took extensive notes, sometimes using whatever piece of paper was nearby or even the palm of her hand. Details were added after our trip to Cambodia in December 1997 and Bree's historical research. We believe our collaboration makes for a wider view and a deeper truth.

—*Daran Kravanh and Bree Lafreniere*

Prelude

This book ventures into the deepest thoughts and memories of a man caught up in an event that led to the death of as many as three million people. While it is a personal, painful recounting of events, the lingering feeling of this story, as I listened and wrote, was one of grace. The complexity of violence and war became clear, and without offering sympathy for the Khmer Rouge, Daran's story revealed their humanity. I began to have a deeper understanding of not only the Cambodian soul, but the search for meaning inherent in the human condition.

This story began with a chance meeting and developed through my need to know life's meaning and Daran's need to recall it. In our work it was as though Daran went under a spell and I was drawn into it.

I begin this story as it began for me, on a September day when, knowing the scale of tragedy in Cambodia, I asked Daran, "How did you survive?" I asked, expecting a few words in return, but the answer was not immediately forthcoming. There was a long silence. I waited and watched Daran's eyes as he searched for an answer.

I
Harmony

I cannot tell you how or why I survived; I do not know myself. It is like this: love and music and memory and invisible hands, and something that comes out of the society of the living and the dead, for which there are no words.

Yes, music, the power within my accordion's voice, saved my life and, in turn, the lives of others. How can I explain this to you? It is strange, this power beyond myself that made itself known to me when I was only a child. This thing with the ability to touch every human being came through music and through myself. It came through my parents, through strangers, and, in the end, through those who sought to kill me and could not.

From the time I was small I loved music. I loved it with a dedication and passion uncharacteristic of a child. All the people of my family were musicians. My oldest brother was a composer and played music from morning till night with a heart that felt no burden. My earliest memories are of sitting on the veranda of our house listening to him play and being unable to sit still. My hands searched for something to tap, to express the rhythm rising within me. Whenever I came across an object—a leaf, a bottle cap—I picked it up to blow into it or hit it to discover the sound of its voice.

Music was not just important to my family. It was part of the daily life of all Cambodians. My people had created songs about waking, departing, reuniting, songs to accompany the preparation for rituals, songs to accompany every life passage. Every action had a song that made one conscious of the moment and expressed something in the action deeper and more meaningful than the action itself.

I know it is not unusual for a person to love music. But when I was seven or eight years old, I experienced something extraordinary. That was the year my parents held a party to celebrate their good fortune and share it with the poor. They organized a feast and invited a group of musicians to come and play so that the people of my province could listen and dance, laugh, and forget their misfortunes.

The musicians arrived grandly in a truck decorated with red hibiscus flowers they had gathered on their journey through the forest. When they jumped from the truck, colorful silk clothes streamed behind them. To me they looked like birds descending from the sky. I knew it would not be an ordinary day.

The musicians went inside my house to rest and visit with my father, and I followed them. I bowed politely and poured them some water. As they spoke with my father, I returned to their truck to have a look inside. There I saw a black box. I wondered what was in it.

I sat next to the truck and watched the village people prepare for the celebration. The men built a temporary outdoor stage of wood and bamboo taken from the forest for the occasion. Women brought cooked chicken and pigs' heads, and colorful fruit heaped in pyramids. They put the feast on a table decorated with flowers and banana leaves. Incense was lit.

I waited for the musicians to return, then watched as one

of them took the box down from the truck. My eyes grew wide as he opened the box and revealed an instrument I later learned was an accordion.

The musician carried the accordion to the stage. I followed him and then stood watching him above me, his face framed by clouds. He was a tall man wearing a white shirt, middle-aged but lively, and he made people laugh. After the musicians were assembled, he signaled them with his eyes and they began to play.

The sound of the accordion entered my world. It was magical—not sound alone but sound accompanied by light and warmth. It was a strange voice, like something far away and at the same time within me. I wanted to get closer so I could see how the musician played it. I climbed up onto the stage. The musician saw me and yelled, "Get down from here, little one!"

"I want to stay," I said. "Remember me? I brought you some water. My father is paying you."

He said, "Oh, yes, I remember you. Okay, you can stay."

So I sat next to the man, watching him with wide eyes and thinking, "Yes, I can do that. Yes, I have five fingers on each hand like him. If we are the same on the outside, we must be the same on the inside."

I stayed next to the accordion player all evening until midnight, when the moon disappeared behind the trees and the people grew full and sleepy and went home. The musicians gathered up their instruments and I followed them back to my house where they would spend the night. The accordion player slept in the room next to mine, leaving his instrument just outside my bedroom door. I lay in bed looking at that accordion, unable to sleep and wondering if I would be able to play it. When I heard the musician snoring, I could no longer contain my curiosity and walked to the accordion. Gently I caressed it while keeping my wide-open eyes on its owner. As I touched it, my heart pounded with a fascination I did not understand. Gathering my courage, I lifted the accordion and carried it to my room, closed the door, and put a blanket under the crack.

The accordion was heavy and the straps became tangled around me. I could not get it to make any sound. Frustrated, I said to the accordion, "Why can't I hear you! Why can't I hear you!" In anger I hit the accordion. And then the latch came loose and its voice was released. I pressed some of the keys and the sound filled me with joy. It was rapture!

I proceeded to experiment with this newfound instrument and after a while decided to play a song. Or maybe there was no decision at all. I played "Svay Chante." And this is the extraordinary part—I played it perfectly though no one had taught me. Perfectly! So there I was—a small boy playing an old Cambodian song on a big accordion. I got so carried away by the idea of this song just appearing to me that I forgot discretion and played without reservation. Music flowed from me like water and released itself into the air and through the walls to the ears of the sleeping.

The musician woke and called to me, "Hey, little one, put that down! I'll teach you to play in the morning." This made me smile. I stopped playing and lay in the dark, waiting for sunrise, but at last fell asleep.

When I woke, my oldest brother Chamroeun was sitting on the edge of my bed.

"Little brother, who taught you to play that song?" he asked.

I did not answer because I did not know. I looked at him in silence and watched a great smile come across his face. He looked at me with the eyes of someone sharing a secret, and I knew he did not expect an answer.

I did not know it then, but an accordion and that song, "Svay Chante," a song about the love of someone unknown, would save me from death at the hands of the Khmer Rouge.

I arrived in this life in 1954. My brown body was built from the fruit of the majestic Cambodian forest, the white rice of the fields, and the clear waters of the Krakor River. My spirit was made of art and laughter, and my soul was composed of many things and many people who had gone before.

My mother gave birth to me at home on a bamboo bed. I arrived quickly with a great gush of water and immediately fell to the ground, scratching my eyelid on the edge of the bed. My mother looked at the blood trickling down my face. Thinking it was a bad sign, she began to cry. But my father laughed and thought it was good. "He will have good eyes, an important thing for a leader," he said and kissed each of my eyes. "And look at his ears! He has good ears, an important thing for a musician." My father was like that. He wanted his children to have an accomplished life.

Nineteen fifty-four was also the year an agreement was being drawn up in Geneva recognizing Cambodia's neutrality in the war that was escalating in Southeast Asia. This was part of Prince Sihanouk's plan to control the Viet Minh hiding in Cambodia near the border of Vietnam. It was also a time of growing nationalism when various political parties formed their identities. What was to eventually become the Communist Party began in 1951, though at that time the leaders were hiding in the forest, spreading their ideas over the radio. The politics emerging at that time was a response to hundreds of years of foreign domination by many countries and the growing discontent of the poor.

But being a young child, I knew nothing of politics. During the day, I helped to garden and sold fish with my mother in the vibrant atmosphere of the marketplace. Evenings were filled with quiet hours of studying the principles of Buddhism and the slow, artful composition of Sanskrit.

My childhood home was a long wooden two-story house that sat high off the ground. It was surrounded by coconut and sugar palms, fragrant flowers, and enormous dark-green mango trees where people gathered to talk, rest, or seek shelter from the rain. The tall trees jutting above the flat land came to represent families. The land was washed clean each day by swift afternoon showers that we could hear approaching from a kilometer away, moving closer and closer like a huge parade of drummers. Those showers were dramatic gifts that woke all the senses and released one from the heaviness of living on this earth.

My house was near the Krakor River. It was a river of life and a river of death: life when it was filled with people laughing, fishing, and gathering fruit brought by the current; death when inhabited by water ghosts who took children as sacrifices. What would come, life or death, we did not know.

I spent many hours playing and swimming at the river with the children of my province. Together we swam in the clear, warm water, then lay in the sun innocently naked. Sometimes we sat together in a circle and made forms in the sand with our bodies. Then we would go around the circle lying down in the impressions others had made—to feel what it was like to be them, living within the confines and shapes of their bodies. It was just a game, but when I think of that time now I see that this child's play was a lesson in compassion.

I lived in Pursat with my father, mother, seven brothers, and one sister. It is not enough to tell you their names or even describe what they looked like. When I think of them, I think of songs. I began to think of them that way when I was young and sat studying upstairs in my house. Listening to the footsteps on the wooden floor below, I found they created little musical pieces. I listened to the songs that were the bodies of my family. I can hear them still: the confident march that is my father; Reatrey, a slow sentimental song; Bunly, a snake charmer's flute; my small sister Raksmey, a lullaby; Sthany, a romantic piece. I hear the rumba in you, Dararith. Samnang, are you jazz? For Rithy a sweet melody. Chamroeun, hands and feet playing together. And my mother a classical piece. And me, what was I? I do not know. We cannot hear the song that is ourselves. That is why we have each other. If I were to guess, I would say I am an old song—so old everyone knows it but no one knows its origin.

All that music surrounding me was harmony. My childhood itself was harmony.

Many childhood hours I played with my brothers. We played soccer and games we made up with materials at hand —lengths of bamboo or sticks or rocks. A favorite of mine was a relay game called "hung." In this game, the first person ran with a baton while exhaling until his breath was exhausted. He then gave the baton to the next person to carry on. The name of this game came from the sound of air being expelled from the lungs.

I was known for my love of sport. I loved movement and action. One year I was chosen to carry a flaming torch in an event much like the Olympics. The torch was relayed from Angkor Wat to Phnom Penh. I ran with it from the temple to a place beyond my house. I remember that the torch was made of metal but it was not heavy. I still recall its scent and the pride I felt as I ran along the red dirt road.

For a time I was interested in boxing. But after a spectacular match when I had bloodied my opponent, my father said to me, "I will no longer allow you to box. I do not want my son to be famous for violence." So I did not box anymore and instead took up karate. I was serious about developing my skill. I remember my father was making a new tile roof for our house. I took some tiles and practiced breaking them with my hands. I broke a lot of them and felt proud of my concentration and strength. My brother saw this and went to tell my father. My father came to me and I feared he would be angry. I waited for his words. He looked at me and said, "Those tiles are very expensive. I would be angry except I see that while I am building a house, you are building character. Character is more important than a house. Just don't break any more."

Though I was surrounded with family, I also spent many hours in solitude on a small island in the middle of the rice field where my grandfather was buried. Lying on the trunk of a tree, I quietly meditated there about the course my life might take. Sometimes I sat under the dangkeap kdam fruit tree and sought my grandfather's advice. The voice I heard from him was not a human voice but one of nature—from that place where my grandfather had returned after his death.

The name of the province where I lived was Pursat. This word *"pursat"* comes from two words: *"po,"* which is the kind of tree where Buddha became enlightened, and *"sat,"* which comes from *"rasat"* meaning "to float."

There is a story about this word Pursat. It seems there was a strange log which floated down the river and got stuck on an island. No matter how strong the current, the log could not be dislodged. Everyone came to see this tree and suddenly, as hundreds of people watched, it broke loose, reversed itself, and floated upstream where it planted itself and grew again. In time the word *"poothisat"* came to mean a person who has dedicated himself to the salvation of others, a bodhisattva, and was destined to attain enlightenment. "Pursat" then came from the word *"poothisat."*

Our house was along National Highway Five. Across the road was a very old temple. I must tell you of this temple because it was very important to my life and to the lives of everyone who lived nearby. This temple was similar in structure to a thousand others in Cambodia: a white cement building with a roof of blue, yellow, red, and green tiles. It had several doors but no windows. Surrounding the temple were statues of ancestral spirits serving as guards, and to enter one had to pass through an elaborate gate with golden birds to the right and left. Inside the temple were many statues of Buddha. Some stared, some smiled, some were bent over in agony. It was a quiet place where hushed words echoed. There all the people of the province held celebrations of life and offered concerts for the gods so they would bring equal amounts of rain and sun to the rice fields.

The name of this temple was "Preach Chay Luong Ban,"

which means "The King Prays to God for Success." There is a story that goes with the name of the temple about a sixteenth-century Cambodian king who had a conflict in his family. The king's two sons could not get along with each other because they both wanted to become king. So one of the sons, Ang Chan, went to Thailand to live with the king there. Ang Chan studied and grew up to be a young man and was much loved by the Thai king. Nevertheless, Ang Chan was not happy. He missed his real father and his homeland, but he knew the king would not allow him to return to Cambodia. So he decided to create a story to convince the king that he should be permitted to go home. Ang Chan went to the king and said, "I have seen the largest elephants! They are white with huge blue tusks. They are heading for the border of Cambodia. Come see!"

He took the king to a place where he had used an enormous log to make what looked like elephant tracks in the earth. The king was very impressed and said, "Oh, I would like elephants like that for my kingdom. Go capture ten of them for me!" So Ang Chan went to Cambodia and was happy to be back in his homeland again. When Ang Chan did not return after several days, the king grew suspicious that his adopted son had tricked him. He sent an army of men to find Ang Chan and return him to Thailand.

When Ang Chan saw the army approaching with their guns and swords drawn, he was certain he would be captured or killed. He didn't know what else to do, so he dropped to the ground and prayed to the protecting spirits to save his life. As Ang Chan was lying there, vulnerable, with nothing to hide him, the army of men arrived. Yet they walked right past Ang Chan, even brushed against him. They couldn't see him. It was as if Ang Chan had become invisible! After the army had left, Ang Chan said, "This place is magic!" So he built a temple to honor the protecting spirits that saved his life and allowed him to be reunited with his father and brother. That is the story of the temple that was next to my house. That is where I had seen the accordion for the first time.

Even after so many years the spirits—the "Neak Ta" they were called—were still strong in that place. The Neak Ta are the ancestors of all the people in a given area who have ever lived there. The Neak Ta in inhabited areas were kind, and you could talk to them. But the Neak Ta in the forests were more powerful, mean, and wild without the living to control them.

How do I know the spirits were so strong? My brother Bunly used to dream of treasures buried near the temple. And each time he did, he would awake and run in his half-sleep to the place he had dreamed of, and dig the ground, and find carved silver arm and ankle bracelets and other such things. He gave them to my mother and she kept them in a locked box.

My brother Dararith was not a believer in the Neak Ta. Once he made the mistake of laughing at the people who worshiped at the temple, calling them foolish. After that, his mouth and face became distorted whenever he laughed. We all knew it was the Neak Ta punishing him, but we could not convince Dararith. He was a stubborn boy.

When I was young I was scared of shadows until once during the night I saw a shadow on my bedroom wall. I lay in bed looking at it, unable to move. Then I began to think, "A shadow is a formless thing, only a dark projection of something else that is not dark. It needs light behind it to make it evident. Even my own body, a thing good and kind, casts a shadow." Such a simple thing, but after that I was not afraid of shadows anymore.

Our people's fear of foreigners began long ago. Our country had the misfortune of being surrounded by the empires of Thailand and Vietnam. Without mountains to the north or south, Cambodia lay vulnerable to invaders who wished to possess the rich land and the labor of the people. Around 1630, a Cambodian king married a Vietnamese princess. As part of the bride price, the king allowed the Vietnamese to establish customs posts in the productive Mekong Delta. Eventually the Vietnamese claimed this land as their own, renamed Prey Nokor "Saigon," and soon the Cambodians living there were surrounded by ten times the number of Vietnamese.

Missionaries from France lived in Cambodia from the beginning of the eighteenth century. In the 1850s King Duang asked for French support to fight off both the Thai and the Vietnamese. The French made an agreement to protect the Cambodians in exchange for teak wood and the freedom to convert people to Roman Catholicism. Although they gave Cambodians protection, they treated them like children. They controlled the king by providing him one hundred kilograms of opium a year. They collected taxes and punished or killed those who did not pay.

In Cambodian culture people are not referred to by name so much as by their relation to one another—such as uncle or brother or grandmother. This is so between strangers as well. I was known by my nickname, Tooch. This means "smallest brother." My parents did not expect to have any more children after I was born. Though they did have more, my designation as "Tooch" stayed with me. But my grandmother never called me Tooch. I reminded her of other people and maybe because she was old and close to death she became confused and referred to me by ancient names.

I did not look like my father. He had curly hair and a square face. My hair is straight and my face round. I did not look like my mother either. My father said my face was reflected in the ancient stone faces of the famous temple of Angkor Wat, hidden in the overgrown jungle of a time long ago. He took me to Angkor Wat once to meet those people, carved in stone, standing as they had for hundreds of years.

It is an extraordinary temple decorated with bas-reliefs of angels, giants, dancers, and figures acting out battles between good and evil. Stone figures with half-closed eyes and half-smiling faces gaze in all four directions.

Of the people in my family, I looked most like my older brothers Reatrey and Chamroeun. The shape of our faces, hands, and lips were the same. My face was the same as Chamroeun's and our souls were the same too. I know this because we could talk to each other without exchanging words. Chamroeun was the brother I loved most. He was brilliant and beautiful and talented. Whatever was in his mind became reality. An idea became a plan, a feeling became a song. He often thought of the future. He made plans for a year at a time. He could speak several languages and loved to read. His room was filled with books on every subject. Chamroeun used to play a game by asking three people to talk to him all at once and ask him questions. While they talked, he did not look at them at all, just hung his head down and listened. Then he repeated back to them all they had said and he answered their questions. Chamroeun could hear many voices at once.

Everyone in Pursat province knew Chamroeun and loved him because he was so kind and friendly. They trusted him because he spoke out on their behalf against exploitation by corrupt businessmen. Chamroeun was special to me too because he was my music teacher. He taught me to play songs from many countries—Laos, Vietnam, Malaysia, and Thailand. All the songs I know I learned from him—all except those I composed myself—but even those he taught me to create so they came from him too. He was so much a part of me, I could never tell in my compositions what was Chamroeun and what was me.

Chamroeun's favorite instrument was the violin. I wanted to be just like him so I tried to love the violin too. But it did not love me. When I played, its sound wasn't sweet. I still blame my violin teacher for my trouble with the violin: I don't think he wanted me to discover the secret voice of that instrument.

One image of Chamroeun especially remains in my mind. When I was just a young boy, I awoke during the night to the sound of music and the creaking of a rocking chair. I looked out the window and saw Chamroeun rocking in a chair and playing his violin. He sang a song to a girl who lived in Kompong Cham province, asking the wind to blow his voice to her, asking her when they might meet again, hoping the day they could embrace would come soon. He played, then stopped to cry, then played again. He rocked in the chair and let his violin cry and began to sing the song all over again. I was just a young and innocent boy who knew nothing of romantic love. But I listened to him sing and instinctively had compassion for his suffering.

One song, called "Koh Kong," always reminds me of Chamroeun. I remember the first time I heard him play it. As he played, his spirit left his body. I could see it go into the sky like steam rising from a bowl of rice. Ever after that, especially when I was alone in my misfortune, whenever I heard that song Chamroeun's spirit would return to me. It made me cry. But after the tears fell it gave me comfort and made me strong. I hear it still and can feel my brother's presence.

My two youngest brothers were Samnang and Rithy. Samnang was bossy and curious. But he listened to my mother's every word and did whatever she said. If someone didn't pay attention to what was being said, they could ask Samnang.

Rithy was my youngest brother. Rithy was motion. He was the only one in the family who did not like to play music. Rithy didn't have time to play music because he was always running. It is that action I see when I think of him.

My mother's name was Chan Hoeun. She was a quiet force in my life. She was not as social as my father but instead worked alone. Being a practical woman, my mother seldom laughed or played with us. My mother was an earthly being.

She was a grower of things, always planting trees or rice or pineapples. Whenever she talked, it was to teach us how to get the greatest yield from our plantings or how to keep the insects away. She was a businesswoman too and took her fish caught on the Tonle Sap to the marketplace to sell for export to Japan, Singapore, and Thailand.

The only time my mother was not of this earth was when she listened to music. Sometimes she would say to me, "Daran, go get Chamroeun and Bunly. I want the three of you to play music for me so I can sing." We would play and my mother would sing and stroke my hair. Sometimes she cried and we would stop playing and ask her why she was crying. She didn't answer but just said, "Play and free my emotions." I watched her face then and could see she was not really with us but instead in some distant place, transported to a realm none of us could know. I now imagine she was thinking of her children. She sometimes spoke of her love for us and her amazement that we had come from her body—that we grew and developed and came then to surround her with the music we created.

I loved my mother, as all children do, but there were times when our ideas were in conflict. I can tell you of one time when this happened. Because we lived along the highway, many people passed by our house. Some came from far away and would be tired and hungry. Sometimes they would ask for water from our large clay jars or fruit from our farm. One day, in sympathy for these travelers, I decided to put a blackboard sign on our veranda saying: "Please, if you are hungry, take some fruit or a coconut." My mother saw this and got the idea to sell fruit to passersby. She told my little sister Raksmey to sit at a table at the side of the road and sell the fruit. When I saw this, I got upset and took the fruit away and gave Raksmey my own money to give to our mother. My mother found out what happened and became angry at me. She said, "If we spend our energy to grow this fruit, we must get something in return."

"Oh, Mother, don't be like that. We don't need the money. We already have everything—a farm, electricity, a radio, fields of rice, hundreds of coconuts, fruit trees, and a bag full of jewelry."

My mother said, "But every penny counts."

"Yes, Mother," I said. "But doesn't Raksmey's life count? Is it worth a few coins to have her sit in the sun all day? That is wasting her time in this life." My mother got furious. Cambodian culture and our Buddhist teachings forbid us to question our parents, monks, or teachers. But her anger left her and she did not force Raksmey to sit in the sun and sell the fruit anymore.

The most important and influential person in my life was my father. If you want to know me, you must first know my father.

I sought always to be in my father's presence, beside his infinitely tall body. I listened to every word he spoke and moved my body as he moved his. Through watching his actions and following his direction, I believed I would come to have, not the knowledge of a child, but that of a man full-grown.

My father was like a god to me. When I greeted him I bowed all the way to the ground—a gesture reserved for the clergy. I disobeyed him only once. It was when I neglected to go to school for a week and instead went to the forest to play music and daydream. I knew this violated all I had been taught, but the yearning was too great for me to ignore. My father came home from work early, however, and heard my music coming out from the trees. When I returned to the house, he asked me if I had just come back from school. I could not lie to my father. I told him I'd been playing music and had not gone to school at all. His face showed anger, but he patiently told me how I must study because it would be important in the course of my life. Now I know it was not my intellect but the spirit contained in my music that would be essential to my survival. My father, of course, could not have known this.

My father once did something, however, that now makes me believe he might have known what was to come. There were a few people in Cambodia called "Nak Such Chung." These people live in the forest alone, wear clothes made from bark, and work and communicate with the animals. I don't know how my father found a man such as this or why he brought him into the civilized life of our house. But the man came, and my brothers and I were told to line up and take part in a ritual that would protect us from harm.

The man took each of us and said, "Don't cry. Sit cross-legged and still as a piece of wood." He then tattooed our bodies with a needle filled with tiger's milk and colored with ink. He made small circles on each shoulder and over our hearts. It hurt very much but I made not a sound. I sat like wood. I became wood. After he had finished with me, he looked into my eyes as if he noticed something, then put an extra circle on my back.

The man was then ready to return to the forest. My father asked him if he would like one of my father's men to go with him to protect him until he reached home. The man laughed and said, "I live in the forest. I don't need protection. I never worry about anything. It is only you outside the forest who need to worry about war and disease or whatever you worry about. I live with nature. I don't worry about anything."

My father was chief of police for our province. His work came out of his deep belief in justice. This was my father's way: when a man was released from jail he sometimes didn't have anywhere to go. In this case my father would say, "Go to my house and work in the garden and make your body strong and your spirit strong and I will aim you for the future." He did this because he believed people were, in essence, good. If they strayed from their goodness, he showed them how to return.

One time a man who had been arrested for attempting to

kill someone came to stay with us. When he was working in the fields he noticed that some of the cows had strange growths on their bodies. He went to my father and said, "I know how to cure that disease." This was a disease that had killed many cows and no one knew how to cure it. My father invited him to try. The man went into the forest to find a particular tree. He stripped its bark and then chopped it up and put it in a bamboo pipe. He went to the cow and lit the pipe and blew the smoke onto the growth. He did this every day and after a week or two the growth began to get smaller until it disappeared and the cow was cured.

My father was very impressed. He advised the man to travel to the farms to cure all the cows afflicted with this disease. "This is your redemption, and this is your power," he said. "Instead of taking life as you attempted to do, you now have the ability to give it back. And do you see that it takes more power to give life than to take it away?" This made the man smile with pride. He packed his few belongings into a folded scarf. My mother gave him a sack of food and he went on his way feeling hopeful and good.

I loved to be with my father. I secretly listened to him talk to my mother before he left for work in the morning. He would say something like, "I must go to Sansar. There was some trouble there last night." After I discovered his plan, I would run as fast as I could in the direction he was going so he would eventually meet me. I'd run, with my small form, back and forth in the middle of the road so he could not pass me and at last my father, a big man in a big car, would surrender and tell me to get in beside him. I would then ride with him, smiling in his presence. When we reached the place we were going, I would stand beside him and watch and listen as he went about the day's work, upholding laws, soothing sorrows, and solving conflicts, so that by the end of the day there was peace and reconciliation. That is how I learned about peace and reconciliation.

My father was famous in our province for his ability to

19

make peace. This is something I once witnessed. Two families lived close to each other; one family had a son and the other had a daughter. Once the boy's father found a letter from the girl in his son's bag. It was a love note saying, "I love you, darling. I want to kiss you one thousand million times" and things such as this. Angrily the father went to his son and asked him if he loved this girl. The boy denied knowing about the letter and said he did not love the girl. The father was sure his son was telling a lie and hit the boy. Finally the boy confessed to his love. His father told the boy, "I will not allow you to love!" He then went to the girl's father and asked him, "Do you know your daughter?"

The man said, "Of course I know my daughter. I know her very well. Why do you ask like that?"

"Has she become a woman yet? Do you allow her to love?"

"No!"

"Then why did she write this?" The man handed over the letter and the girl's father read it and became furious. He went to his daughter and picked her up by her shirt. He asked her, "Do you love this boy?" She, like the boy, denied everything.

The two men were very angry at their children but agreed they would watch them carefully and not allow them to attend the same school.

Three years went by and then one of the fathers found another letter describing a love deeper than the first. He became uncontrollably angry and went to the other father and said, "This is your fault! You have not been watching your child!"

The other said, "Yes, I have. It is because of you this happened!"

They argued loudly, then began to hit each other. The wives came to stop them but the men only pushed them out of the way. When the men finally stopped, they were beaten so badly they both had to go to the hospital. The nurse at the hospital called the police and that is how my father got involved.

I was at the police station that day, so I rode in the car with my father to the hospital. He met the men and their wives and said, "I should arrest you for this, but I do not want to put you in jail." My father was a police officer but he hated to put people in jail. He said to them, "After you heal, I will come to meet you and help you solve this problem."

A week or two later I went along with him and two of his men to meet with the families. Before we left the police station, my father told one of his men to take his flute and instructed the other to take his drum. They did so without question because they had come to know the ways of my father. We all got into the truck and went to visit the families. When we got to the house my father did not talk about the problem. Instead he told some jokes and two stories and shared some ideas about how to improve the rice crops. Then he suggested his men take out their instruments and play a song to dance by.

The music made them forget about their trouble and the two men danced first with their own wives and then, at my father's urging, danced with each other's wives. When they stopped, one said, "Sir, we thought you came here to solve this problem."

"Oh, yes," said my father, "I forgot."

I smiled because I knew he had not forgotten at all, but I sat quietly and watched. My father asked the parents to bring their children to meet with us and suggested the couple have a chance to dance together too. They were confused. The parents urged them to go ahead, so they danced together through several songs. After that they sat down and my father began to talk.

"You are close neighbors. You've always helped each other and never had any conflicts. Now you see love has happened between this boy and girl. Love is a gift from nature. Nature made boys and girls differently so they would need each other. And they are old enough now to love, so we must respect nature and allow them to love."

My father's words did not please the two fathers. One of them said, "You can talk about love but I am still angry. My face is still swollen."

The other replied, "I too am still angry. You hit me hard and accused me of lying!"

The whole argument started again. My father came between them and said, "Stop! You complain about the pain in your body but that will go away. In time, when you die, your whole body will go away and your life will not continue —not unless your children have children and that cannot happen until first they love. That is what is happening now. This conflict you see is only life calling. But if you prefer death, if you want to be forgotten, that is your choice. You can hate each other. But I suggest that you have a respect for nature and a love of life. Put this conflict aside and think of your family and the future."

At last the two men surrendered and the conflict ended. The boy and girl were married a year later in the most elaborate wedding anyone could remember. And the following year they had a boy child whom they named Kong By, my father's name.

In a family of so many boys my one sister, Raksmey, was very special. I still hold a memory of her. When I was sixteen or seventeen years old, my father had to go away on a military exercise and left me in charge of guarding the family. The Khmer Rouge had started guerrilla attacks so I slept outside on the veranda. I was armed with a 16-mm gun, a pistol, and grenades.

I should not have worried about the Khmer Rouge. The danger to my family came not from guerrillas but from inside the house when a kerosene lantern fell over on Raksmey and her face and hair caught fire. She had fallen asleep while reading a book. I was sleeping below her room, but the smell of smoke awoke me quickly. I kicked open the locked door and ran to Raksmey's room to see her sitting upright, tall flames coming out of her head. My mother and Sthany came, too, and tried to put the flames out with their hands. I smothered the fire with a blanket, but Raksmey's hair and one of her ears were burned off. My mother's hands and arms were badly burned, as well, though in her fear for her child she did not notice her own pain.

My father had gone to lead an army of men in a military exercise on an island in the Tonle Sap. Word of Raksmey's misfortune reached him just as the ship was leaving the port. My father, without thought, abandoned his men, jumped into the water, and swam to shore. He ran in his wet clothes, jumped onto a truck loaded with chickens, and finally reached the hospital and embraced Raksmey.

Raksmey liked to study. She liked reading and writing. She had lovely handwriting and always took first place in school. Her grades went down, though, after her hair burned off. She cried when she fell to fifth place. My father consoled her saying, "You are still beautiful and smart. You will always be beautiful and smart."

Telling of my father brings his face back to me. I loved him so much that my mind is full of his memory. My father was so bright and wise he could make those in despair happy again. I saw this with my own eyes. There was a man in our province who was always unhappy. He drank too much and got into fights and tried to seduce other men's wives. My father arrested him many times. After a while, my father took pity on the man and invited him to our house to live with us. The man came to stay with us in the peace of our farm, but still he was unhappy and could not carry on with life. Several times he tried to kill himself. Once he threw himself under a car but the tire missed him. Another time he jumped from a tall building but did not even break one bone. Each time this happened my father counseled him by saying, "It is not your fate to die yet."

Finally one day when the man again tried to kill himself, my father said, "Okay. You want to die? I will kill you myself. Today. Do you want to die today?"

The man was surprised that someone would say such a thing but said yes.

"Are you sure?" my father asked. "You can't seduce women or drink alcohol when you're dead."

"Yes, yes, I am sure," said the man.

"Okay. I will kill you now."

I knew my father was not a violent person, so I looked in disbelief as he loaded his gun, took a rope, tied the man's hands, and put a blindfold over his eyes. My heart was beating wildly. I followed them through the forest where my father stopped to cut down a banana tree. We walked to the river's edge and my father stuck the banana tree in the place where the land dropped off into the water. He then tied the man to the tree and asked again, "Are you sure you want to die?"

The man said, "Yes. Please, kill me."

My father put his gun near the man's shoulder and began shooting, not at the man, but at the tree so at last the tree fell, with the man, into the river.

I watched as the man's body broke the surface of the water and I looked at my father to see what he would do. He did and said nothing. He waited a minute or two and then jumped in to save the man. He pulled the man onto the shore, then pumped the water from the man's chest. When the man caught his breath, my father removed the man's blindfold and asked him, "How do you feel?"

"I feel wonderful. I feel as if I have been reborn," said the man. "Thank you, Kong By."

After that the man was happy and never again drank alcohol or touched another man's wife. I later heard he survived the war and an outbreak of cholera and lives in Cambodia still, talking of how my father killed him and gave him a new life.

In Cambodia, teachers have great responsibility for shaping the character of a child. Certainly my father believed this. When I was old enough to go to school, he brought me to my teacher and said in the traditional way, "Here is my son. Leave only the bones." While my teachers taught me many things, it was my father who gave me straight strong bones.

Much of what my father taught me I learned at my family's weekly meetings. My father always began these meetings by saying, "You are my advisers, and you are my mirrors." Then we would resolve all the week's conflicts and take turns advising my father and each other in a thoughtful way. If we did not give useful criticism or show proper understanding or compassion, my father would say, "You are not being a mirror, only a glass."

During these meetings we practiced our music and had discussions. During the harvest season the meetings were preceded by a harvest ritual. In this ritual we spread rice stalks in a circle and then some of us would play music, always a song called "Saturday Happiness," while the others danced on the rice stalks to separate the grains from their husk. We danced until we were exhausted and empty and ready to be filled again.

Many of the conversations from these meetings still remain in my head. I remember my mother saying, "Daran, you killed ten birds this week. It is not good to kill so many birds."

"But what of you, Mother?" I replied. Every week, with one sweep of your net you kill hundreds of fish. Yes, fish are smaller than birds but their life, that life within them, measures the same. That is true, Mother."

Another conversation has returned to me many times over the course of my life. It occurred during a meeting in which my father announced, "I tell you today that I believe Daran is the representative of our family." My eyes widened at the words. My older brothers protested and asked, "Why should

Daran represent our family? We are older than him and have more education."

In answer, my father said to them, "Why? Let us look at his character. Why does everyone love Daran? What, in Daran, produces love? Why whenever visitors come from far away do they want to see Daran first? Why is it so quiet and lifeless in our home when Daran is not with us?" After a few minutes, my brothers and my sister gave their answers in turn:

"Because he is beautiful."

"Because he is wise and saves his money in a box."

"Because he raises pigs and chickens and gives the money from their sale to others."

"Because he plays music very well."

"Because he loves justice."

"Because he is a good soccer player."

"Because he always gives half his rice pudding to me."

"Because he is like moonlight in the dark."

And my mother: "Because he is my eternal child."

My father was the last to speak. "Daran is my best mirror. He makes me see myself. So you see," he said, "Daran must be the one who represents us and we must try to be as he is." Everyone agreed. They looked at me but I did not know what to say. I was a small boy and wondered how I could possibly carry the responsibility of representing my family. My fate, however, would show the way.

This part of my story would not be complete unless I told you how I came to have an accordion. And if you want to know how I survived the holocaust of Pol Pot, that too relates to my accordion. This is how it happened that I received an instrument which was to save my life.

In 1963 Chamroeun went to dance and play music at a celebration in which Prince Sihanouk was the honored guest. When he returned home he told me he had seen the most beautiful accordion. It belonged to a musician of the prince and Chamroeun wanted to buy one for himself.

After some weeks, he made the trip to Phnom Penh and returned with his new instrument. I looked at it and loved it instantly. I wanted to play it but Chamroeun would not allow me. He thought I was too young and only knew how to play one song, "Svay Chante." He told me, "I don't want to hear 'Svay Chante' over and over again!"

In my desperation to play, I decided to pretend I was sick so that I could stay home from school and play his accordion. The next morning, after everyone left, I took Chamroeun's accordion out of its case and played it all day. I was delirious. I walked around the house eating fruit and doing whatever I wanted, holding that accordion and saying, "I am the king now!"

Many times after that I stayed home from school to practice the accordion. I began to observe and listen carefully to my brother's music, watching the rhythm of his breath and how he moved his fingers.

Then one day, while Chamroeun was playing the violin for my mother, I picked up his accordion and joined him in the song. He and my mother grew quiet and looked at me in surprise. Chamroeun called to our father, "Come, look at your son!"

Later, when our parents had left the room, Chamroeun asked me how I had learned to play so well. I said, "I am smart like you."

My brother said, "No, Tooch, I don't think so. I think you've been staying home from school so you could secretly play my accordion."

"No, I have not," I said.

"Don't lie to me, Tooch. I know because I found my accordion in its box upside down and you can't close the lid tight like I can."

After a minute I said, "Yes, I lied to you. But I must. If you do not allow me to play, I must lie because I must play."

At that moment our father came into the room. I pinched Chamroeun and whispered, "If you tell Father, I will hate you my whole life!" Our father asked us what the matter was. We told him, "Nothing."

"Don't say 'Nothing,'" he said. "I know when there is conflict in my family."

My brother and I didn't say anything. Then our father said, "You don't want to talk? It doesn't matter. I already heard everything you've said. I want to tell you now this is not Daran's mistake and this is not Chamroeun's mistake. This is my mistake. It is my mistake because I am the one who should provide for all the needs of this family and I have neglected to provide something to my child which he needs like water and food."

My father went off somewhere and did not return until midnight. When he got home he woke everyone up and told us to go to the big room. My brothers rubbed their eyes and complained that they were tired, but I did not mind the awakening. When I entered the room I saw a round table and in the middle of the table was a box wrapped in blue paper. All around this box were candles flickering in the dark. When everyone had gathered around the table, my father said, "I want you to guess what is in this box. Bunly, can you guess? Reatrey, can you guess?" He asked each of my brothers in turn. He came to me last. "Tooch, can you guess?"

I said, "Yes, I can guess. I guess it is an accordion, and I guess it's for me!"

"Yes," my father said laughing.

I opened the box to find an accordion. I took a deep breath. To my delight, it was not an ordinary one. It was a beautiful one, the kind belonging to the king's musician. I held it in my arms and it reflected the light from the candles in the middle of the dark room. I stood with this accordion and was surrounded by my family and I was inexpressibly happy. My father and mother hugged me and said, "This belongs to you now. Play it, our sweet son. Play it with all the love we have given you."

"Yes, it belongs to me now," I repeated, and I played a little song.

We all returned to our beds and the house became silent as my family slept. But I lay awake in bed with my accordion for a long while playing every song I knew. Near dawn, I closed my eyes. As I fell asleep, I was filled with a kind of peace that no measure of misfortune or suffering could destroy. And that was good, for there was much misfortune and suffering to come.

II
Discord

There have been two dark periods in Cambodian history. The first was in the fourteenth century when the spirit of Cambodia is said to have disappeared like water evaporating in the sun. Indeed the water did disappear and the canals became clogged. The rice would not grow and the people died the slow, ugly death of starvation.

I lived in Cambodia during the other dark period, the reign of the Khmer Rouge, which was a time darker than the first. Indeed there was so much terror that even the protecting spirits of our ancestors ran in fear. Fate put me in a country in the midst of a war of ideology that did not take into account the innocence of childhood. By the time I was fourteen years old, I had seen war with my eyes and had inhaled its bitter scent through my nostrils. But even before then, at ten, I had a basic understanding of injustice and conflict.

It is difficult to say when the trouble in Cambodia began. It was slow and quiet at first. Maybe it began long ago when the war over control of the waters was fought. Maybe it began with the invasion of the Indians, the Chinese, the Siamese, or the Vietnamese—or the arrival in the 1850s of the

French. Maybe it began with the idea of Rousseau's "noble savage" or Mao's "Great Leap Forward." Maybe it was the rising of youth against their elders. Maybe it began with hunger—or the fear of strangers, or jealousy, or simply the evils within men. Historians perhaps would say that Cambodia's trouble began in the 1930s with the idea of nationalism or with the education of Pol Pot who would later lead the Khmer Rouge. Maybe it was all of these things put together in the mind of first one and then seven million Cambodian people. I do not know. I am Cambodian, but I do not know. I only know that in 1975 the light and spirit of Cambodia went out and would not return for many years.

Let me tell more about my country's history. In 1953, Cambodia gained independence from a hundred years of French colonial rule. For a thousand years before the French, a series of kings ruled: King Jayavarman, Indravarman, Najendravarman, and Yasovarman. The role of the king was to protect the people against foreign enemies and the forces of nature. The suffix *"varman"* means "protection." Kings were actually called god-kings because the people believed their rulers obtained their power from the spirit world. The kings were seen as superhuman. Dust and sweat did not stick to them and they had no scars.

The kings ruled almost invisibly. On rare occasions they went out to remind the people of their greatness. The king was preceded by hundreds of palace women wearing flowers in their hair and carrying candles or golden bowls. Following them were ministers on elephants, shaded by red umbrellas. Next came the king's wives and concubines in carriages or on horseback. And then the king appeared, standing on an elephant and holding his sacred golden sword. In front of his audience, he acted out rituals to make him appear to be the hero of Indian epics.

In modern times, politics became very complicated. There were factions within each political party and numerous combinations of ever-changing alliances. Politics was a contest of personalities—a contest not of written documents but of spoken words and flowery language. It had more to do with showmanship than with the daily life of the people. Indeed, most people lived in the countryside and followed the rhythms of nature and the ideas of Buddha, not politics.

In 1941 the French hand-picked Prince Norodom Sihanouk to lead the country. The French took advantage of his age, just twenty-one, and largely controlled him. But he was also very popular among Cambodians. In time he developed into a charismatic leader with talents as a songwriter and a movie producer. He was, it seemed, a friend to everyone. He flew in his plane over the villages and threw bales of clothing and candy out the window to the peasants below and they loved him even more. It seemed God loved him too. For everywhere Sihanouk went, rain and a good rice crop were sure to follow.

This devotion to Sihanouk began to change during the 1950s after independence from France. Many political parties started to make themselves known. Among those seeking to gain a following was a group of young men and women who had studied in France. One member of that group was a man named Saloth Sar, later known to the world as Pol Pot. With training from the Vietnamese Communist Ho Chi Minh, the leaders of the new Communist Party began to introduce their ideas to the Cambodian people through radio broadcasts from secret locations and newspapers written by journalists with no names. They criticized Sihanouk for his excessive wealth and his support of foreign intervention in the affairs of Cambodia. Some found the Communists' ideas good and true.

In 1960 there was a national congressional meeting of the Communist Party, known at that time as the Revolutionary Army of Kampuchea. During that meeting a man named Tou Samuth was elected secretary-general. Soon after he was elected, he was murdered and Saloth Sar, who had been deputy secretary, became secretary-general. The year before, the editor of the Communist newspaper had been killed as well, and the murder of these two leaders created a cloud of mistrust of Sar and his followers. Sar reacted by taking himself, his men, and his ideas into the small villages of the forest.

Deep in the forest, cut off from the rest of society, the Khmer Rouge leaders formed their identity and recruited people for their cause. They set up networks of spies including women and children. Most of the people who joined them were poor peasants—mostly young, uneducated, even illiterate people, unhappy in their poverty and jealous of the upper-class elite of Phnom Penh. Vietnamese and Chinese Communists taught the Khmer Rouge how to find people's point of weakness. If they were poor, the Khmer Rouge gave them money or goods until the people came to trust them, became believers, and followed them blindly.

The Khmer Rouge studied without books and trained themselves by killing animals. They did not emerge from the forest until 1968. When they came out they had a vision for Cambodia that required vast, radical changes in society. They wanted to expel all foreigners and any ideas that did not have their origin in Cambodia. They wanted to return our country to its agrarian roots and make it completely self-sufficient. They wanted to do away with class differences, Buddhism, and private property. They were prepared to fight for what they believed in.

This struggle for revolution started with guerrilla units formed to carry out acts of terror. The Khmer Rouge began to execute low-level government leaders and local chiefs in public and dramatic ways. The first uprising was by the peasants in 1968 in Battambang province in northwestern Cambodia. From there the violence spread and became more visible and more brutal. The peace and harmony of my childhood was replaced by civil war. My life and that of my fellow countrymen began to disintegrate.

The Khmer Rouge continued to recruit cadres in the rural areas. But as they overran the villages, the thousands of people they had not recruited fled to the cities. The population of Phnom Penh tripled. With so few people working in the rural areas, rice production fell dramatically. Food prices soared and there were protests in the streets. In time the Khmer Rouge became more militant and outspoken. They continued to recruit people for their cause. They appealed to people's sense of injustice and played on the exhaustion people felt at fighting a civil war. Their theories and passion were convincing to some, including my father's brother. I remember debates between the two of them.

One day at our weekly family meeting, my father said in a solemn voice, "The war is not just in Vietnam. It is in Cambodia too. And Laos. It is a war surrounding us, in all of Indochina. Someone we cannot guess is organizing this war for reasons we cannot know." He told us that in the event the war grew closer, we should fight and could be certain that in the end good would win. He wanted us to be leaders of a new Cambodia, a Cambodia that was just and peaceful. He told each of us how we could bring about that peace. We trusted our father and agreed to do whatever he asked of us.

In early 1970, Sihanouk left the country to vacation abroad. During his absence, there was a bloodless coup and Lon Nol, backed by the United States, became the leader of our new republic. We were all hopeful that our lives would become peaceful and prosperous, but the Lon Nol regime clung to the old ways of corruption. The government spent increasing amounts of its resources fighting the war.

My personal experience with the Khmer Rouge began in 1971 when my brother Chamroeun went to visit our grandmother and his fiancée Sophat, who lived near the Tonle Sap. But that area was a training ground for the Khmer Rouge. By then Chamroeun was a famous businessman and journalist who had publicly criticized the Khmer Rouge. He was captured and held hostage for a month. They put him in a jail made of bamboo, tied his arms, and beat him with a stick.

My father was the commander of the Republican forces stationed on a ship on the Tonle Sap. When word arrived that Chamroeun was being held hostage, my father negotiated for his release. When that did not work, he said he would send in a plane to bomb the area. After that Chamroeun was set free and walked through the bush to the lake. My brother looked terribly thin and dirty after his ordeal. When no one at the lake would lend him a boat to row out to my father's ship, he jumped into the water and began to swim. The men on my father's ship spotted him. Thinking Chamroeun was the enemy coming to plant a mine, the men asked our father, "Should we shoot him?"

My father looked at the figure in the water and hesitated. He said, "No, don't shoot. That looks like my son." Chamroeun came closer and was helped onto the boat where he fell in front of the men. My father said, "Yes, that is my son. It is good we did not shoot." That is how terrible it was in Cambodia in 1971—one could hardly tell the difference between one's enemy and one's son.

In 1973 the Khmer Rouge radically changed the life of the people under their control. They abolished ownership of private property and formed agricultural cooperatives. Everyone was required to wear black clothes, the symbol of a peasant. People living in the Khmer Rouge areas were not allowed to become monks or wear jewelry. Religion and vanity were considered counterrevolutionary. During that time I was a college student living in Pursatville, thirty-two kilometers from my parents' house. As my education and experience increased, I found I was inflamed by injustice and made articulate by suffering. I became an outspoken leader and was elected student body president at the school. I began to speak out about all that was happening in my country. The students responded to my passion.

I cannot say I disagreed with everything the Khmer Rouge were saying. I know now, as I knew then, that they were correct in criticizing inequality and corruption in Cambodia.

But the Khmer Rouge were violent and extreme and had an uncompromising vision for our country. They wanted cultural purity and unity, but their ideas for such unity required absolute obedience from all and I feared for those who opposed their ideas. That fear made me speak out against a Khmer Rouge government.

I fought for ideas or against ideas, not political parties. I also fought against corruption by government officials. One official in particular was notoriously mean and corrupt. One day my brothers, some other students, and I decided we could not allow this man to take advantage of our people any longer. Planning to kidnap him and then insist that he be fired from his position as commander of the military police, we went to his villa. When he emerged, I walked up to him and said, "I want you to come with me."

He laughed at me and said, "Who are you?"

"I represent the people and we want you to resign your post."

"Get out of my way!"

I stood in front of him and blocked his path. His face got red with anger and when he reached for the gun on his hip, I kicked him. At once the other students standing behind me came to help tie him up and then we put him in the back of a horse cart.

The commander's men saw what had happened and called the police. When they arrived, we began negotiations for his release. The police asked us what we demanded. I said, "We demand that this man stop raping women. We demand that this man stop taxing fifty percent of a poor vendor's sales. We demand that this man stop taking bribes from Chinese businessmen who don't pay any taxes at all."

As more people gathered around to give us support, the negotiations grew more intense. A helicopter flying over the whole scene caught the attention of my father who had come to watch, but he did not intervene. When the government and the police saw that the people supported us, they gave in to our demands. Before we released him, however, we pulled the horse cart around so the people could line the streets and he would have to face the people he had betrayed. Though some wanted to hit him and throw rocks, we protected him because we wanted no violence. We simply wanted peace and justice. I believed at that time that everyone in Cambodia, like people everywhere, wanted peace and justice. But no one could agree on what was just, or how to arrive at peace, so the war continued.

Those years were a time of major change in our society. Cambodia had been, for thousands of years, a Buddhist country with ideas of justice unlike those in the West. The concept of equality clashed with the traditional concept of karma, which teaches us to accept the life we are given. These conflicting ideas were much debated. The debates separated people, even brothers. Hatred and mistrust spread and began to consume our lives.

By early 1975 life in Cambodia had no order. Rice and sugar and other staples became unaffordable. People were without food and medicine and began to steal from one another, and the soldiers stole chickens and cows and rice that should have sustained the people. Meanwhile the fighting between Lon Nol's Republican government and the Khmer Rouge intensified. The Khmer Rouge planted mines on the national road. They wore the black uniforms and caps of the Chinese, hid in the forest, and shot at vehicles going by. The war got closer. My neighbors were dying. Every time I went out, I saw blood and people being carried off to the hospital by frantic relatives. I began to carry a gun.

My father was still stationed on the Tonle Sap. He wrote me letters saying his men were dying but he didn't want to give up. He missed me, worried about me, and begged me to be careful. "Tooch," he said, "beware of the Khmer Rouge. They look like you and me, but they will kill you without hesitation. They are clever."

My mother wrote, too, asking me to come home. Everyone was returning home, seeking trust and comfort from those they knew. I missed my parents, but I was not yet ready to come back home. I was too stubborn—and besides, the injustice I saw around me gave me the energy to fight. I did not know the situation could grow even worse.

In late March of 1975, Chamroeun came to see me. He told me he had been leading groups of civilians to fight against the Khmer Rouge. He was thin and nervous. He was hoarse from shouting so much and almost voiceless. He whispered painfully, "Tooch, the situation is hopeless. Stop thinking about society. Think only about yourself. I am going home to take care of my wife and my children. You should go home too."

I told him, "No, Chamroeun, I must stay. I want to organize a thousand students to fight." He argued with me saying they had already tried their best to fight. "Brother, please believe me," he said. We hugged each other good-bye and cried with the deep sadness that the uncertainty of war creates.

At that time the capital, Phnom Penh, was surrounded by the Khmer Rouge. It was a city that had been established as the capital in 1866 at the insistence of the French, replacing Angkor further inland. They saw Phnom Penh's proximity to the South China Sea as strategic to world trade. By 1936, half of the city's hundred thousand people were Chinese or Vietnamese, many of them merchants. The Khmer Rouge saw Phnom Penh as a breeding ground for capitalists and foreigners.

At the beginning of April 1975, foreign embassy staff and those of the upper classes abandoned the cities. Others stayed and armed themselves with guns. Radio Phnom Penh broadcast the speeches of unidentified Communists who spoke of liberation, justice, and independence. Some people began to believe that at last the war would be over and there would be peace in Cambodia. I was not so sure. I decided I would continue to fight. I still believed that the Khmer Rouge could be defeated. There were reported to be only sixty thousand in their army in a country of seven million people. I spoke with the students of my school and persuaded them to keep fighting. I went to see the president of the school to ask him if we could provide the students with weapons. He was uncooperative and his staff argued with me. "Please," I said. "This is not the time for us to quarrel with each other. This is the time to be united."

"No," the president said. "This is the time to wait for the new regime. Daran, just go home and sleep. That's all. That's all."

How could I sleep? I lay in bed listening to the sobs of the woman living above me. I grew tense listening to the howling of hungry dogs abandoned by their fleeing owners—such a haunting sound. I felt a strong sense of impending disaster.

After a few days, some students and I tried once again to speak with the military officials to get their support. We went into their office and found them dressed in the black clothes of the Khmer Rouge. They held up the Communist flag and told us, "It is time to submit to our new government." We refused. We left and I told everyone, "If you see the white flag of surrender, tear it down!" But some had become scared, others hopeless. I saw people I knew go into the forest and come out wearing the black clothes of the Khmer Rouge. I said to them, "You look strange. It's as if I don't know you."

On the day of April 17, 1975, a radio broadcast stated: "Everybody, drop your guns. Say hello and welcome the Khmer Rouge." I said, "No! No! No! No!"

I ran to talk to people I knew and said, "We cannot allow this to happen to our country. We must fight!" They didn't want to listen. They had grown tired and had given up. Hopelessness had changed them. Many went out into the streets to wave and welcome the Khmer Rouge parading the streets of the city. But the soldiers looked strange. They did not have the smiling faces of liberators but the cruel faces of men seeking revenge.

Even with their victory, even with the triumphant parading, the war against the Cambodian people continued. The soldiers entered the capital and immediately expelled the two million people living there. All the people and all the life drained out of Phnom Penh and the beautiful city with its white buildings, wide boulevards, and its temples and palaces then lay empty.

In Pursatville soldiers walked the streets. They went into the stores and put everything in bags. They went into every house, even the hospital, ordering people to go to the countryside. The soldiers said to them: "Don't take your possessions. The new government will provide you with everything you need." Those days were so chaotic. Nobody knew just where to go or what was to happen.

Even at that time I did not want to give up. On April 18 I went back to speak with the president of the school. When I reached his office, I was told he had been taken to the forest and that the Khmer Rouge would be holding a meeting with the students momentarily. They had been holding meetings with different groups of people all day—first military personnel from the Lon Nol government, then professional people. At those meetings, people were told the rules of the new society and instructed to leave town and go to the forest.

I joined a crowd of two thousand students gathered to hear what was happening. The Khmer Rouge explained that they would restructure our society to eliminate imperialist influence and class differences. They told us they had built new schools in the forest and we were to go there to study. Someone in the crowd, a military officer, got angry and walked up to the spokesman and challenged his ideas. The soldiers listened impatiently for only a moment, then one of them said to him, "You must follow our directions now. You are no longer an officer, so take off your stripes!"

When the officer refused, the soldier ripped the stripes off the man's uniform, put a gun to his head, and shot him! The man fell onto the platform. Blood ran out of his head and dripped down. There was a collective gasp from the crowd. The Khmer Rouge soldier said, "Now, does anyone else want to protest?" Everyone scattered. Sickened by the coldness of what I had just witnessed, I walked away.

But that was just the beginning of the brutality. The Khmer Rouge continued killing innocent people. Some of the women became hysterical as their husbands were taken away and their homes pillaged. They ran shouting into the streets, where the Khmer Rouge shot them and pushed their bodies into the river.

On April 23 my two younger brothers, Dararith and Sthany, came to see me. They had ridden on a bicycle all the way from Chamroeun's house thirty-two kilometers away and arrived breathless and sweating. Sthany said to me, "Brother, it's too dangerous now. Please come with us back to our parents' house." I agreed because I had just witnessed another execution of an officer behind the governor's residence and was beginning to feel scared and hopeless about stopping the Khmer Rouge.

I filled a backpack with my books and the three of us climbed on the one bicycle. I pedaled while Dararith sat on the back seat and Sthany stood behind me. Suddenly impatient to get home, I pedaled as quickly as I could through the crowds fleeing the city. I still see people's panicking faces, the old and the sick being carried by others. I still hear the sound of crying babies. People's possessions were abandoned on the road—furniture, photographs, silk clothes, statues of Buddha—as people began to realize only their life was worth saving. The day was strange, unreal, like a horror movie. The humidity was oppressive, the wind scented with gunfire and death, as though nature reflected the mood of the people. I felt a heaviness in my heart and breath.

My brothers and I rode along a road lined by forest. In

my fear, these trees took on the monstrous faces of a child's nightmare. I was a strong person and had never cried in my childhood. But on April 23, 1975, I began to cry. Sobs escaped from my chest as I thought of the uncertainty and darkness of our future. It was fortunate my brothers were behind me and could not see me cry. I wanted them to think there was nothing to be afraid of. But I am sure they could sense my fear.

After pedaling for about ten kilometers, I grew tired. I had not been able to sleep for several days and had hardly eaten anything. But I kept thinking of my family and was anxious to see them, so I did not stop to rest. As we rode further, we began to see people going in the opposite direction —coming out of the Krakor district of Pursat province. I saw someone I knew and called to him, but he did not stop. So I turned and rode along with him. "What's wrong? What's happened?" I asked. "Have you seen my family?"

"Yes. Your mother gave me these cakes to give to you." He threw the cakes to me.

"What about my father? Did you see him?"

"Yes. The Khmer Rouge came for him and told him he has to go study in the forest for a long time."

I stopped pedaling. Turning the bicycle around again, I headed in the direction of my home. Suddenly I felt a terrible fear and longing for my father. Maybe I no longer had a father. I felt lost and alone like an orphan. Then I began to think, "Where is my little sister, Raksmey? Where is Chamroeun? Where is Bunly? Where is my littlest brother, Rithy?" Thinking about my family made me stronger and I pedaled faster so I might see them sooner.

As I continued to pedal, I saw more and more people coming out of Krakor district. I looked for my family among the faces, but I did not see them. People shouted to me, "Turn around! There is nothing left."

"No!" I shouted. "My father is there. He can take care of

me. And my mother and my farm and the temple and my grandfather's grave!"

No one was listening. It was as if people were deaf, consumed with their own fear, thinking only of their own survival.

We were about five kilometers from my parents' house when we were stopped at a Khmer Rouge checkpoint. They were ordering people to throw away their money. "It is unnecessary in our new society," they said. I did not believe them. I picked up the money and put it in my pocket. One of the soldiers came closer. "Where are you going?" he demanded.

"We are going to our home in Krakor," I replied.

"You're not allowed to go any further," he said. "Turn around and go that way." They looked at our clothes and our backpacks. "Are you students?" the soldiers asked, looking at each other and laughing sarcastically. "In that case you can go study in the forest. Go that way."

I argued with them. "No, we must go to Krakor! My father is a commander there."

One of them pushed his gun into my chest and shouted, "He is not my commander!"

I dropped the bicycle and my two brothers and I ran away. We ran until we could not see the soldiers anymore. We rested and then began walking again.

I cannot describe the feeling I had at that time. We were walking without knowing where we were going or what was to happen. We were scared, lost, and hungry. My brothers said, "Tooch, we are hungry and thirsty." I gave them our mother's cakes which by then had broken into pieces. When night came, we stopped to sleep in a rice field. It was not a comfortable place. It was wet and cold and the ground was covered in manure. I told my brothers, "Don't worry about that. Just sleep and dream."

We walked for another day and came to a place where a man and woman were selling noodles and dessert. I bought all they had with the money I had picked up and asked them to make some more. I told my brothers, "Eat! Eat! Make your bodies strong." Before long some soldiers saw the smoke from the fire and came over to the vendor. They said, "Capitalism is no longer allowed," and they shot at the pot with their guns. My brother Dararith started to cry. I held his small hand. We walked away while the vendor stood there shaking.

As we walked, we came across people going in every direction—thousands of people. Everyone shouted to each other, "No! That's the wrong way!" Every way was the wrong way. No one knew which way to go. We simply went in the opposite direction of gunshots, like cattle being steered into the slaughterhouse.

We walked through the forest toward the north, crossing National Highway Five. It was so dark we could hardly see where we were going. I held tight to Dararith's hand. We walked and periodically I would call out to Sthany, "Brother, are you there?"

"Yes, Daran, I am here," he would reply. Over and over I repeated, "Sthany, are you there?" and I heard him say, "Yes, I am here." But once when I called to him he did not answer. I called and called his name, but there was no voice in return. There was only silence.

I stopped walking and sat down and hugged Dararith close. I continued to call out to Sthany, but his voice did not return. It must have been about two o'clock in the morning and poor young Dararith was exhausted. He slept on my lap until daybreak while I cried and wondered what had happened to Sthany and what would happen to Dararith and me.

The next morning, my brother and I walked to the west until we came to an area where some five hundred people were gathered. The Khmer Rouge soldiers seemed to be trying to bring order. They were setting up tables and talking with each other. Families were clinging together or holding onto the possessions they had managed to save in their flight. Some people sat silent and sullen; others argued.

The soldiers gave us some rice and water, and while we ate they told us of their plans. They said that our lives would be better. They said things like, "We are in control now. The long war is ended. Angkar will provide for you." *"Angkar"* is a word meaning something like "government." Everyone wanted to trust the Khmer Rouge and believe them. And perhaps we would have, but when a baby began to cry, interrupting the soldier's speech, the soldier grabbed the baby and threw it to the ground.

The soldiers began to separate people into smaller groups. They told a group of us to go to a place near a temple. Vulnerable and afraid, we did as we were told. The soldiers began to ask questions. One asked me how old Dararith was.

"Eleven," I told him.

"Then he can go over there," the soldier said, pointing to a corner of the temple.

"Please," I said. "He is the only relative I have now. Let him stay with me so I can take care of him."

"That's not necessary. Angkar will take care of him."

"Who is Angkar?" I asked.

"Angkar will take care of all of you. Angkar will give rice to you. Angkar will give duties to you."

They took Dararith away and put him with a group of children and they were led away. He looked back at me, crying uncontrollably, and called "Brother! Brother!" I stood helpless to comfort him.

After a short while the soldiers announced, "If any of you are military officers we will increase your rank by one and send you to another place to study. Are there any military officers here and what is your rank?"

Some of the men who responded were told to stand together. Then the soldiers asked the rest of us, "Who are you?" I thought I would lie and say I was a farmer, but I was dressed in the white shirt and khaki shorts of a student and still had my backpack filled with books. "I am a student," I said.

"Then go stand over there."

I was put with the group of military officers and some other men who had fled Phnom Penh. The men were all educated people—engineers, doctors, teachers, military officers—and because of their education I knew they were considered enemies of the Khmer Rouge. I became increasingly uncomfortable and asked a soldier, "What will you do with us?"

"You will be sent to study in the forest," he replied.

When the soldiers left to talk to some people, I said quietly to the other men, "This is strange. I know this province and there aren't any schools in the forest. I don't think they can build schools so fast. Maybe they really want to kill us."

One of the others said, "No. The war is over now. They won't kill us."

"I don't know," one of the men said. "Maybe they will." He thought for a moment and then continued, "I cannot die. I have a wife and four children to care for. I don't want to be separated from them." He started to shake and cry. Then we all began to think about the separations from our families.

"My brother, I am sorry," I said. "But I think they want to kill us. They are not concerned about our education. If they were, why not use the universities and colleges already built in the cities?"

Someone said, "Oh, you think too much!"

We all wanted to believe that the war was truly over. But thinking about the preceding few days did not make us feel hopeful. I said, "We don't know if the Khmer Rouge will help us or kill us. Let's be careful. We don't know the future."

A man who identified himself as a major said, "Yes, it is possible they want to kill us. But if so they will tie us up first.

In that case, we need to fight back. If they take out some cloth to tie us, look at me—and when I wink, start fighting them."

One of the doctors said, "Oh, I cannot fight. You can see I am fat and not very strong. You can fight for me."

Someone else said, "No, that is the wrong idea. We need to help each other now." We all agreed and sat quietly. We watched the soldiers smoking cigarettes nervously.

After a time, six soldiers approached and told us it was time to go. Anxiously we rose and formed a single line. I ran over to where Dararith was. I hugged him and said, "Try to stay in this place. When I have a chance to come back, I will. Take care of yourself. We don't have our parents anymore. Remember!" A soldier came over and grabbed me. He yelled, "Hey! Go with your group!"

I returned to the group and the soldiers ordered us to start walking into the forest. There were eleven of us, and I was at the end of the line. Away from the others, the soldiers suddenly pointed their guns at us. We walked for an hour and stopped to rest, then walked another hour. As we walked deeper into the forest we saw many more soldiers and our fear increased.

Then suddenly the soldiers leading us pointed their guns at us and shouted, "Put your hands up!"

They took red strips of cloth and began to tie us at the elbows. We looked at the major but he didn't wink so we didn't fight. I wanted to fight. But I could see there were so many more soldiers than us and they all had guns. We were tied and marched single file past that group of soldiers and then for another kilometer or so.

As I walked, I was flooded with the terror of knowing I was being taken to my death. I was only twenty-one years old and I was going to be killed by my fellow countrymen simply because I was a student! I could not believe my fate. I did not want to die. I searched the skies for strength and guidance.

At that moment I heard my father's voice. He was not really there, but I could feel him standing behind me, tapping my back and saying, "Are you open yet?" Suddenly I was hurled back into a vivid memory from my childhood: a ritual to gather strength from the king-master. I wore the ancient style of silk clothes and sat on the floor with my family sitting behind me. A large group of musicians played traditional music while my brothers and I meditated on the sounds. After a long while my parents prayed to the king-master to enter me and make me strong and brave. They said, "Please, we invite you king-master, god, angels of heaven and earth, spirits of the forest, and brave heroes. Enter our son and protect him from harm." Sometimes it took hours for me to open up to allow the king-master to enter me. I knew he was within me when I saw a white circle in front of my eyes and I felt myself transformed, not small anymore.

I remembered my father tapping my back and saying, "Are you open yet?" "Do your eyes see clearly, or not? Does your nose breathe in the air to give you strength, or not? Can your voice shout to scare your enemy, or not? Do you feel brave, or not?"

"Yes! Yes! Yes! Yes!" I had replied.

I returned to my present danger. Silently I repeated the request to the king-master in the Cambodian language:

> Prah vey vongsa moha cham puu
>
> Samdech prah kruu
>
> Nak such chung khantey
>
> Prah eysey, eyso, sar champa
>
> Oknah kleang moeung
>
> Chumteav khan khiev

I begged my family to stay by me. "Please," I said. "Gather around me and give me your strength." In my mind I practiced the techniques I had used in karate and boxing and I felt stronger. Rising within me I felt the will of youth: the will to survive.

After we walked a while longer, we came to a sight that provoked fear in all of us—a massive hole in the ground intended to be our grave. I could smell it before I could see it: the smell of sickeningly sweet earth just turned to make room for death. The man at the front of the line panicked when he saw the hole and turned to run. The soldiers quickly shot him. In the confusion, I kicked one of the soldiers. I did not wait for a signal from the major.

Then we were all fighting for our lives. Some of the men tried to run away but were shot by the soldiers. We were now in dense forest, however, and the soldiers could not raise their long AK-54s to shoot accurately, so the men's wounds were not fatal. As I kicked one soldier, his gun went off and the bullet pierced my hand. I was stabbed in the side of my knee and hit in the throat with the butt of a gun. We continued to fight for what seemed a very long time. We fought until all the soldiers were dead or nearly so.

It seems impossible to me now that we could have overcome the soldiers. They must have been surprised by our determination. I was surprised by my own strength. But I know it was not merely my strength but that of the king-master too. After our struggle, we lay stunned and exhausted. Blood covered our bodies and the ground. We were dazed with the suddenness with which our country and our lives had changed and shaking from being so near death.

We rested only briefly, then took the clothes, guns, and supplies from the soldiers. We put on the black clothes of our enemies and stood looking at ourselves and each other. The other men and I pushed the bodies into the hole that had been intended for us and, without any sense of where we were going or what was to become of us, we turned and walked deeper into the forest.

Front left to right: Daran's mother; Reatrey holding Samnang; Daran's sister, Raksmey, being carried; Daran; Daran's father; Sthany. Bunly is on the far right, second row. This photograph was taken at Daran's family home in 1965.

Daran, a few months before the Khmer Rouge takeover.

Daran *(right)* with his one surviving brother, Reatrey, at the site of their childhood home. December 1997, Cambodia. (Photo: Janet Jensen)

Fence posts built by Daran and his father and brothers. (Photo: Janet Jensen)

III
Bridge: In the Forest

When I think of my life in the forest, I think of falling rain. Even now, many years later, I cannot listen to the slow, steady sound of rain without being drawn back to that time. The sound of rain brings to my mind an image: I see a group of men sitting in a circle, not exchanging words but only the warmth and security of each other's bodies, and waiting in silence a seeming eternity for the gods to intervene and change their fate.

When I think of my life in the forest, I think of my thin body fighting against a wind sweeping across Cambodia like a sad human moan. Whenever I heard the wind coming, I'd kneel down on the ground so the wind wouldn't knock me over. Because to get back up would take all the strength I had. Near the end of my time in the forest, I feared that just one more wind—so innocent, so benign, so comforting under normal circumstances—would kill me.

When I think of my life in the forest, I think of hunger, the only reality, burning like alcohol on a wound. The forest was rain and wind and hunger. But more than that it was a place of suffering and, ultimately, a place of transformation.

After our encounter with the soldiers who tried to kill us, the ten of us walked painfully and silently through the forest. We came to a cave where we took shelter. There we cleaned each other's wounds by wrapping a stick with a piece of cloth and plunging water into the wounds. This caused agonizing pain and our collective shouts reverberated into the empty sky, falling on the deafened ears of God and a humanity too far away or too indifferent to hear. We wondered if the world knew what was happening in Cambodia. Surely someone would learn of our fate and come to help us.

We stayed in the cave for several weeks and debated what we should do. At first we thought we would leave the forest and fight the Khmer Rouge. But after days without proper food or water or medicine, our strength began to dissipate. We thought perhaps after we were healed we would try to escape to Thailand.

In those early days, we sustained ourselves on the food we had taken from the soldiers, which was not much more than rice, and whatever leaves and berries we found nearby. We took turns going out to look for food and water, but mostly we stayed inside the cave. In that darkened atmosphere, there was little indication of night or day and we lost our sense of time. In the dark we could barely see each other's faces. It was as though each man's form dissolved and disappeared and all that was left was his voice and the energy escaping from his body. Our conversations then were like talking to ourselves. We talked of fear, hunger, and pain. We cried for ourselves and for Cambodia. We listened to the sound of the dripping water that had carved this enormous hole in the rock. We sat and thought about the future.

As a boy, my brothers and I had explored caves. But living in a cave was different. It was like going into the center of the earth or to the depths of my own mind with all the images it contained. It was like returning to the beginning of time. Indeed, my companions and I were starting life again with nothing at all. We were stripped to the nothingness of Buddhist monks or dead men.

We did have each other, though, and we were fortunate to have two doctors in our group. They knew how to find medicinal plants in the forest to heal our wounds. Honey became our salve, certain leaves stopped the flow of blood, and bark became the painkiller for our broken bodies. The doctors made an antibiotic by mixing a particular root with water in an indentation in a rock. We took turns sipping it and it made us feel better.

Both doctors were light-skinned Cambodians of Chinese descent. Like the other men they wore glasses. The other men were much older than I. One was a primary school teacher. He was a man about fifty years old, small and soft-spoken, meek, even. There were two professors. One, a teacher of math, was thin with a happy disposition. In the early days he tried to make us laugh at our misfortune, though he was seldom successful. The other professor was a teacher of philosophy.

Two of the men were engineers, one of whom was very dark-skinned, even darker than most Cambodians. Among us also were a major and a lieutenant—or at least that is what they told the Khmer Rouge. When I came to know them, I thought perhaps they were not really officers. The major could not speak French, as all well-educated people could, and he could not read the map very well. But their former identity made no difference. In the forest we were merely men, equal, as the Khmer Rouge had wanted us to be, equal in our sadness and misfortune.

Though I lived with these men for a year, I never learned their names, nor did they know mine. It was not important to us. We referred to each other as "doctor" or "teacher" or whatever we were. I was the youngest and was referred to as "Tooch," little brother, as I had been called in my family.

After a month, our wounds were almost healed and our supply of food had run out. We left the cave in search of food and water and hoped we might make it into Thailand. In our discussion of who should lead us, the major spoke loudly. He was mean and strict and liked taking charge. After some debate, the major convinced us, in his authoritative voice, that he should lead us because he had a compass and a map. At the time this made sense, though we came to find that these objects of science offered us no direction. They knew nothing of the danger of mines, the desperation of men, or the strange situations that would confront us.

At that time we were near the Tonle Sap and about a hundred kilometers east of Thailand. We knew a national highway led to Thailand, but of course it would be heavily patrolled and dangerous. The only other way to Thailand was through a dense forest over the high Phnom Kravanh mountains to the west. That is the way we began.

We had become used to the relative security of the cave and felt vulnerable in the forest. The vegetation was dense and this, combined with our weakness, caused us to trip easily. Falling and bumping our unhealed wounds caused us great pain. The thick brush made numerous hiding places for enemies. Our eyes and ears were on guard every minute for the black uniforms of Khmer Rouge soldiers or the slow, heavy step of tigers. From the time Cambodians are small, they hear stories of the forest. We have folktales of people being abandoned in the forest. The stories tell of struggles to avoid its darkness because that is where wild animals, malarial mosquitoes, and evil Neak Ta dwell. I felt like a character in one of those stories.

We had trouble sleeping without shelter. The nights were cruel with no bed to lie on, no blankets to cover us, and no light but that of the moon. The nights were cold and full of danger—tigers and snakes. And there were dangers inside our heads too—nightmares and the seductions of death.

We spent our days walking west looking for water and food. We lived on fruit, leaves, and potatoes. We dared not start a fire lest we call attention to ourselves. I tried not to think about anything except food and water. We believed it would take two weeks to reach Thailand, but the way was not easy. For one thing, we didn't have enough food. Often we got lost and would stop to argue about which way to go. We had many quarrels. Some of the men wanted to throw away the guns we had taken from the soldiers because they were heavy, and we argued about that. We would walk in one direction for a while and then hear mines exploding. Or we'd come upon a Khmer Rouge camp, then turn and go in the opposite direction. It was exhausting and discouraging.

My efforts to think only about my physical survival began to falter. I began thinking about my family all the time. I remember whispering, "Where is my mother?" When I did so, a song came to me and I began to sing: "Oh mother, oh mother, I wish you were by my side." Cambodian people cry when they hear that song. It is from a sad movie about children lost in the forest. The children call for their mother and their voices reach the trees, reach the leaves, reach the air, reach everything except their mother's ears.

I knew that eventually I would have to accept my circumstance and somehow find peace. Away from the others, I asked the sky: "Before, I had a house, a family, food. Now I have nothing. Who has put me in the forest to live naked and hungry? Where is my family? How can I survive? Is it better to die? What fate awaits me?" Though I had no answers and I found no peace, I knew one thing. It was not my time to die.

When we did not have the strength to walk, we sat quietly in thought—or without thought if our thoughts were too much to bear. After being in the forest for weeks with so little food, we did not have the energy to do more. Sometimes we sat together and drew maps in the earth with a stick to help us decide which way to go. Each man told the others what he believed was the right way. No one knew for sure. We followed our intuition more than anything. But our intuition was often wrong and our way was blocked by soldiers or by nature. Sometimes we sat alone and drew pictures of food and smiling faces and the names of those we loved. We would look at our drawings, meditating, and finally sweep them away with a brush of our hands so we would not die of longing.

At night we built a trap in hopes of catching a rabbit or a deer. The trap also protected us from tigers. We went to sleep waiting for the sound of a catch. When we heard the sound, we immediately prepared to eat, whatever the hour.

We had agreed to share whatever food we could find. But after a time, when we became more desperate, the temptation to hoard food was almost irresistible. Once I discovered by chance that one of my companions had been hiding food. I was lying alone at the base of a tree when I heard a woodpecker drilling the tree. Soon a mouse came and tapped the ground around the base of the tree, which produced a curious sound. I wondered why the tapping sounded so strange —like a drum. I pushed the brush aside and found some slices of dried potato in a hole. I told the others and there was a big dispute. No one admitted their guilt and after a time it made no difference. We divided the potato and it gave us some relief from our hunger.

Day after day passed and our bodies grew thinner. We began to think, not about the past or the future, but only the next few minutes when we might find something to eat. Often we sat with our eyes closed because it took too much energy to keep them open. Our speech, when it emerged, was slurred and slow. When the rain came we did not have the strength to seek shelter. Instead we just huddled together to seek warmth as water poured over our bodies. We were beginning to believe we could not make it out of Cambodia and wondered how long we could stay in the forest.

Despite all the rigors of living this way, I remember moments, mostly at nightfall, when my mind was at peace. Every day one person was assigned to sit high atop a tree to watch out for soldiers making a sweep of the forest or to look for others hiding from the Khmer Rouge who might join us. Ascending the tree was a nightly ritual usually given to me because I was the one with the most strength. As the light faded, I would gather lengths of bamboo, sharpen the ends, and then pound them into the tree so that I could climb them like a ladder. That is the way my father had taught me. This preparation had a rhythm for me, a beautiful rhythm like that of my body and a song of my father. After I reached the top of the tree, I would connect vines from a branch to the wrists of the others sleeping below so that a shake of the branch could alert them to danger.

I loved that assignment—sitting quietly, being the caretaker and the eyes for my friends. It was in those moments before sunrise that I felt happy. At daybreak, perched high above the earth, the world looked peaceful and kind and beautiful. I saw bamboo groves with great expanses of earth on either side. I did not see war. In my mind I saw only the great blue Tonle Sap brimming with fish, great mountainsides of shiny marble, and caves filled with gold. I thought of my beautiful Cambodian people, their dark sensuous grace. I saw them dressed in silk and dancing ancient dances, their long hands and fingers telling stories or inviting love. I thought of my sleeping companions below who looked like young children before they learn of cruelty and sorrow. I imagined their dreams of food and loved ones long lost, and whenever in their nightmares they awoke, I tugged lightly on the vine and sang them back to sleep. It was there at the top of the tree that I composed a song. Though I did not have an instrument or any paper or pen to record it, I did have my mind and my voice. I still carry that song in my mind.

Sitting in the tree was not always peaceful. Once when I was watching from a tree, I saw a group of black-clothed Khmer Rouge coming toward us. My companions were cooling off in a pool of water. I dared not shout my warning to them. Instead I climbed down the tree quickly and threw rocks at them to get their attention. We ran away and hid in a shallow crevice of rock behind a waterfall. We were scared and tried not to make a sound. My heart beat frantically. Two of the soldiers came close to us. One of them walked within a foot of me, so close I could feel the heat from his body, but he did not see us. I thought of the story of Ang Chan, who had become invisible to the king's army.

Then one of the soldiers fired his gun, so the major jumped out and shot both soldiers. We came out from behind the rock to take the supplies from the soldiers' bodies. It was then we saw a deer lying nearby. We realized it was the deer they had been shooting at, not us. So we took the deer and hid before any other soldiers could find us. Though we were happy to have meat, the image of dying men had reappeared before our eyes, reminding us there was still war in Cambodia.

More days passed, weeks, months, and our bodies somehow grew thinner still. Our clothes were thin and torn and I had lost one shoe. I replaced it with a leaf. Our hair grew so long and snarled that if we had had a mirror we would not have recognized ourselves. Our emotions grew wild—at once desperate, confused, and sad. A desire for death was mixed with our instinct to live. As I lay down to sleep each night, I breathed deeply and sighed slowly. "Ah, today I survived."

Under the hot sun of Cambodia, our search for water was constant. In this quest we were helped by an ancient story.

Long ago there was a master called Ta Aisay, which means "Patient Grandfather." He was a very old man with a white beard, and he carried a cane. One day the master called two people to him, a woman named Maykala and a man named Ramaso. He said to them in his shaky, quiet voice: "I offer you a challenge. I will give you each a special glass. The first person to fill it with dew will receive the power of magic."

Maykala and Ramaso accepted the challenge and went on their way. Ramaso went to a big field, put his glass on the ground, and waited for the dew to fall out of the sky into his glass. He lay on his belly and looked at the glass for many days.

Maykala did something else. In the early morning, she went into the forest and gently shook the dewdrops off the leaves into her glass. She was quick to fill her glass and return to the master. The master rewarded her with a little ball which gave her magic.

Days later, after Ramaso had filled his glass, he went to the master and demanded the power of magic. When the master refused, Ramaso became jealous and angry. He stole a magic hatchet and ran away. Later he met up with Maykala and they quarreled over who was most powerful. When Ramaso began to chase Maykala, she flew up into the sky and he followed her there. As they approached each other, Ramaso's hatchet hit Maykala's ball and the combination of these two magic powers created thunder and lightning. Rain fell over the earth then, and ever afterwards.

The men and I collected water as Maykala did: by tapping leaves covered in dew and allowing the water to run into our mouths.

Stories helped us. Indeed we searched for anything that might help us, including animals. Once we came upon a tree with a fruit none of us had eaten before. We watched as a monkey ate the fruit. The monkey ate it without any ill effect, so the doctor tasted it. "It is sweet, so it's safe to eat," he proclaimed. We were overjoyed. I thanked that tree for giving me another respite from death by starvation. "Thank you! Thank you," I said bowing my head, hands together in respect.

But not long after we ate the fruit, we all became horribly sick with vomiting and diarrhea. Between my convulsions I cursed at the tree and shouted, "I thought you were giving me life, but you've only tried to kill me!" When I looked at that tree, it was no longer a tree but a foreboding shadow with a plot to poison us. For days afterward it seemed no life remained in my body.

This incident nearly destroyed the solidarity of our group. The major got very angry at the doctor. He shouted, "You said it was safe to eat that fruit and we nearly died!" He attacked the doctor and hit him in the face. I threw myself between them. The doctor pushed me and said, "Go away! I will handle this!"

"Wait," I said. "If he had wanted to kill us, he would not have eaten the fruit too."

"I told you to go away!"

"Could I just stand here behind you to see how you solve this conflict?" I asked.

"No! Get out of my way," said the major and he pushed me aside.

"But I want to see how two brothers who need each other can solve their differences."

The major looked at me without saying anything. One of the other men said, "Major, our little brother is right. We need each other."

The men were looking at the major and finally he let the doctor go and walked away.

I think the other men began to look at me differently after that. Though I was the youngest in the group and the men had never sought my advice before, they began to do so. This respect increased when I returned to the group one day with a deer to eat. I had gone out to look for food and was unable to find anything. I got tired and sat down on a grassy hill. To entertain myself, I played a little song by blowing into a folded leaf. The sound drew a deer out of the forest. I was excited at the thought of eating some meat, but I didn't shoot the deer immediately. He was a full-grown deer—"a father probably," I thought, "looking for his children and thinking the sound of my leaf was his children calling." I talked to him. "Why are you so afraid of humans? Do you know instinctively they will kill you? Is that why you live in the forest, far from people?" I kept looking at him and debating with myself, "Should I kill him? I am so hungry. My companions are starving and I have a chance to provide them with food. If we don't eat, we will die."

I said to the deer, "How can I kill you when you are someone's father, like my father, with a wife and children and a desire for life?"

Long silent moments passed. Finally I said, "Deer, can you sacrifice yourself for us? We don't know how to live in the forest and we are not ready to die."

The deer did not answer me. He only walked closer and stood before me. I raised my gun and shot him.

After his life disappeared, I returned to the others with the deer on my back. When they saw the deer, they shouted with happiness and thanked the spirits. And while I too felt gratitude to something beyond myself, it was the deer's sacrifice that I gave thanks for.

Later I returned to the hill to play my leaf and wait for a deer. But this time the sound from my leaf drew not a deer but a tiger. Suddenly I was the one facing death, and I ran for my life. After that I never knew if my song would draw a deer or a tiger—and whether I or a deer would be the sacrifice.

Months went by. It was the hot season and water was hard to find. As we walked through the forest one afternoon looking for water, we suddenly came upon a man sitting in meditation. He was old and had long hair and a beard that reached to his stomach. A stone bowl of water was next to him. Coming upon such a sight in the middle of the forest was surprising and we halted and stood in silence.

"Let's ask him for some water," said one of us.

"No!" said another. "Maybe he is a soldier in disguise."

"He can't be. He is too old."

"He's really strange. Maybe he is a ghost."

"But he has water and I'm so thirsty."

"Why is he sitting here away from everyone?"

"Maybe he is studying and seeking something."

"Yes, maybe he is a monk. Let's ask him for water."

"How does he support himself?"

"This could be a trick of the Khmer Rouge."

So the debate went on until we decided that thirst was our gravest problem. We went closer and said to the man, "Hello, kind sir. May we have some of your water? We are so thirsty." The man did not move. He sat quietly, cross-legged, with his eyes closed. He hummed. When we spoke again, louder this time, he opened his eyes but did not speak. He pointed his finger at the water. After our incident with the poison fruit, we all were afraid of this water. One of the men said, "I will try it."

He sipped the water slowly and we asked him, "How does it make you feel? Do you feel any burning, any dizziness?"

"No, no. It is good," he said. And he drank it for a long time, but we did not see the water level go down. The water seemed to be replenished as quickly as it was being drunk. Then we all took a turn. I sipped slowly at first, then took great gulps. I never tasted water so sweet. I felt my blood thin out and begin to flow smoothly.

Who was this man? We were never to know. He would not or could not talk. And although he pointed to markings on a tree and a rock, we did not recognize the words and could not make any sense of them. The man spoke not a word, but his presence showed us that we could survive in the forest. So we left him sitting there and went on with renewed confidence.

When the rainy season came, the nights became uncomfortably cold. I dreamed of a time in my childhood when I was wrongly accused of harming my brother Sthany. My mother wanted to punish me and asked the police to come and arrest me and put me in jail. It was cold and dark in the jail and I cried all night. I asked the air, "Why am I being punished for something I did not do?" When the morning light appeared, I heard my father's voice. I called to him, "Papa! Papa!"

"Who is that?" he asked.

"It is me," I called.

"Me, who?"

"Me, Tooch."

"Tooch?"

My father came and picked me up. He looked into my eyes and asked, "What happened?" He looked at his men. "What is the meaning of this?"

"Your wife, sir. She asked us to put your son in jail."

"This is a child!" he roared.

"Yes, we know, sir. But your wife . . . this is a special case."

I awoke from this dream calling for my father. When I saw that I was alone in a dark forest and he was not there, I curled my body around itself and cried as if I were a child.

I missed my family so much that when I thought of them I was filled with an enormous emptiness. The missing was mixed with worry and fear for their fate. I especially missed my father. I remembered that when he used to go away, he would take beeswax and put it in my hair. He would say, "I want you to forget me for a while and live in the happiness of the present. I don't want you to think of me until I return and can reunite with you." In the forest I followed bees, hoping they would lead me to the beeswax that would help me forget my father. But the bees were too quick and went to heights I could not reach.

At that time I had not yet accepted my forest home. I felt my humanness too much and felt set apart from the life of nature. But this attitude changed suddenly one day when I climbed a tree to pick some fruit and there, in the top of the tree, I saw some fish. These fish, known as *ksan,* were in a pool created by a huge round plant that attaches itself to the tree and fills with water when the Tonle Sap overflows into the forest.

I looked at the fish a long time. Finally I said to myself, "If fish can live in a tree through some force of nature, I can live wherever fate puts me." I then came to accept the circumstances of my life.

Living with nature in the forest with no house, no bed, nothing, can be very difficult unless you recognize its beauty and surrender to it. After I surrendered to my fate, I saw my world differently. I saw the beauty of its order. I saw the artful arrangement of rough red leaves on delicate green ferns, flowers in vases of stone, berries in perfect geometric patterns—the whole of it reflected in hundreds of dewdrops. Everywhere, especially in the rainy season, new was springing from old, life was springing from death.

That Cambodian forest was beautiful. It was grand to have a house covered in green carpet soft on bare feet. Marble walls. Carved staircases. I was provided with paintings and sculpture. There was music—symphonies of birdsong, wind in the trees, harmonies and choirs. I wondered if those animals knew they were in harmony with one another or if each believed he was alone. In the forest there was theater and drama, too, the whole story of life acted out for me. I was the audience for the rituals of mating, migration, growth, the fight for survival, death, and rebirth.

I found many valuable things in the forest, even sapphires and emeralds. One day the engineer found some diamonds in a rock. He got very excited and started jumping up and down until his pants fell down. The professor of philosophy said to me, "Look at that man. How does he have the energy to jump up and down? How does happiness create such energy? How does power come from paying attention to a rock? Why doesn't he go look for a leaf to eat instead of jumping at the sight of a rock?" We both wanted to laugh but neither of us had the energy.

He was right, of course. When you live in the forest, diamonds lose their value. They are no more precious than anything else. It is all the same: the life, the value, of everything is equal, is as important as the next. Even my human life was equal to that of a fly eaten by a frog in the eyes of a tiger who knows only hunger, which was the same burning hunger as mine.

This same hunger, though, could blind me to the forest's beauty. When I was desperately hungry or thirsty, beauty had little value. I remember a waterfall cascading into a pool of water lilies that was extraordinarily beautiful. Yet I looked at that waterfall and saw only water to drink—water that would keep me alive a little longer so my heart would continue to beat. Life meant my voice could create another song, my mind could have another memory of a day lived upon this earth. I drank that water and received another chance to discover the meaning of my life. Water made that possible.

This idea of the value of food and water was introduced to me by my father. But it was only after living in the forest that I understood. I remember my father talking to us while we picnicked one day. He playfully said to us, "Does anyone here see any gold?"

We all looked around and said no. And my father said: "You must see it. It is everywhere!"

"Where?" we all cried.

"You are sitting on it. You are eating it."

"What do you mean, Father?"

"It is simple and easy to understand," he said. "This ground and your food are gold. They are the most valuable things. Why? Because the ground gives us food to put into our bodies and this allows us to live and have children and go on into the future. That is gold. Life is gold, more valuable than anything."

My father, he knew. He knew everything.

So you see I began to change. I believe the point when I was transformed came on the day I began to understand the chatter of birds.

This happened while I was lying on the ground, looking up at the sky, listening to the songs of a bird. I wondered, "If I sang like a bird, could I fly like a bird? Is it their music that gives them flight?"

I watched as a mother bird left her nest to find food for her young. I heard her say, "I think I will take that leaf for my children. There, there, little ones. I have enough for all of you." I allowed myself to become that bird and soon I was flying across that great expanse of sky—a sky without soldiers to stop me, without borders, without hidden dangers. I felt the sweetness of freedom and was released from my sorrow.

When I returned I looked at those birds, not really with my eyes, but as if through a telescope. And when I lay on the ground and looked at the earth, I saw everything from a different perspective: close enough to experience the slow, peaceful crawl of a worm, close enough to see its heartbeat and its struggle—close enough, that is, to feel compassion for a worm. After I felt that compassion, I was not the same. I was adopted by nature. I was now part of nature.

My companions noticed this transformation in me. One day we were sitting together when a lizard appeared. "Look!" I said. "It is my grandfather come to help us!"

"Oh, little brother! What are you saying?"

"That lizard, he is my grandfather. Let me tell you how I know. When I was ten years old, my maternal grandfather died. My father and my uncle buried his body near a rice field. They made a grave in the shape of a circle and laid his body down in it. It was beneath a tree that attracted many birds with its hundreds of tiny fruits. After my grandfather's death, my mother cried endlessly and nothing we did would console her. Then, when it was time for the Hundred Day Celebration signaling the time when a person is reborn, we all went to the grave and set out food for my grandfather's soul. While our eyes were closed in prayer, a lizard came out of the tree and ate some of the food. When we opened our eyes, my mother saw that some of the food had been eaten and she cried, 'Father, you've come back to life!' The lizard came to stand by her side. This convinced her that her father had been reincarnated as a lizard who lived in the tree towering over the circle where her father's body had been laid. And every time we went there we called for him, 'Father!' 'Grandfather!' and the lizard appeared.

"So you see," I said to the men, "he has come here to help us now." During the time it took me to tell this story, my companions forgot their suffering. Somehow they believed me, and believed in the lizard, and felt a little better.

After these incidents with the birds and the worm and the lizard, the creatures of the woods became my friends. Birds sang the songs I requested. They told me stories. One time I was walking alone looking for food. I had searched from morning until evening and could find nothing to eat. I decided to return to the others with this unfortunate news when I came across a dead bird on the ground. I stopped to look at it. Maggots were crawling in and out of its rotting body, but its head was still beautiful and unbroken.

I pulled the bird's head from its body and held it in my hands. I returned to the men and said, "Here, I have brought you some food."

They looked at me like I was insane. Even so, I started a fire and cooked the bird's head. I divided it into ten sections and put each tiny bit into the mouths of my companions. They ate it and one of them said, "Yes, brother, I feel stronger now." Then we slept and the next day we all felt better than we had in a long time. It was only a small thing but contained such power!

If we had been birds we could have flown out of the forest, across the border, beyond the reach of guns. But we were men. And all but I would die, three in the forest and the others later.

The doctor was the first to die. He died without warning. One morning he did not wake. I saw he was dead and thought perhaps he had died of hunger. When I lifted him, I saw the mark of a snake's fangs on his back and the track of a snake on the forest floor. I called to the others and we gathered around our friend. We realized we did not know his name or anything about his life. We were sad but did not have the strength to cry or bury him. We laid him on a rock, made a pillow for his head with small branches, and wished him well in the next life.

One of the professors was the next to die. This happened a few months later when we were looking for water. I remembered a time when my father had taken me to cut vines for a swing. He had pointed out a vine that was filled with water. We were searching for that vine when the professor got separated from the group. Later we heard him shout, "I've found some more water. Oh, come see this! Baby tigers! They are . . ."

Then we didn't hear his voice anymore. We called to him but he did not answer and he did not return. We walked in the direction where we had heard his voice and found him about ten meters away. His scalp had been ripped off and it lay covering his face. His body was bloody and one of his arms was torn off. He was dead.

We stood stunned, nauseated, and unable to move. Someone started to walk to the body, but another one shouted, "No, stop! This is dangerous! Let's go back!" We ran away leaving the professor's body there alone. For a time after that, I believed death was bound to be the inevitable victor. Death's presence hung heavy over me. During that time I often thought to myself, "If only I had my accordion, I could survive." I missed the comfort it gave me.

Leaning against a tree, I remembered the time when I did not go to school for a week but instead spent every day going into the forest to play my accordion. Leaning against a coconut palm, I had listened to the wind blowing the tops of the trees and had imitated the sound on my accordion like an echo or a duet. I had played love songs and been filled with longing for a girl I had known. She was half-Cambodian, half-French, and used to pass below my window on her bicycle. Whenever I was playing my accordion, she would stop her bicycle and hide behind a tree to listen. She never spoke to me, nor I to her. We only felt each other's presence and let the accordion's voice express our thoughts.

Remembering this while hiding from the Khmer Rouge made me determined not to surrender, not to the soldiers, not to death. I wanted to go on with life. I wanted to see the face of this woman and know her love. Memory and longing pushed me on.

After we had been in the forest for a year, we knew we could not survive much longer. We were near the border of Thailand and wanted to seek safety in that country. But the border was heavily patrolled by the Thai authorities and the Khmer Rouge, and the area was planted with land mines.

We sat at the edge of the forest in a place where we could see Thailand. How could we make it across the border? It seemed hopelessly dangerous. We agreed we could not risk it. Even so, one of the men, the lieutenant, decided he could not go back in the forest. He said, "I cannot live that way anymore. There we will surely die. Crossing that border is our only hope. I am willing to go first. And if it means I sacrifice my life, I am willing to do that."

We tried to persuade him not to go but he was stubborn,

so we hugged him and told him to be careful. He set off. We watched. He did not go far when a mine exploded and killed him. So quickly! I felt breathless. The teacher began to cry. We stood there a while and then we debated. Now that the mine had exploded, was the path free of danger? Was there more than one mine? What if we followed the footsteps of the lieutenant exactly? And who would go first?

The major finally decided we all must go. I protested. "Are you ordering me to die? Can you order me to be reborn? If you can't, I will not go."

As we debated, a rabbit ran across the border and another mine exploded. "See," I said to the major. "There are still unexploded mines."

For two hours, we debated. Finally the major said to me, "Brother, you are the youngest one. You must respect the rest of us and be willing to go first."

"But you are older and more experienced, so you should go," I replied.

"But you are younger and stronger, you can run faster," he said.

"But you are a military man and the model for the rest of us."

Back and forth we went until the major grew furious. He grabbed a gun and put it against my chest. I reached for a gun too and we stood pointing our guns at each other. I was so weak I could not hold the gun for long. It dropped out of my hand and the major came closer and pointed his gun at my head. "Go!" he said.

What could I do? I had to go. I looked at the sky and asked my parents for protection. I asked the king-master to enter me. I closed my eyes and imagined my father close by. I visualized the danger ahead. I saw death standing nearby, but I also saw a hundred good spirits of my ancestors. I imagined meeting an enemy and holding my sword and stick to protect me.

When all was clear in my mind, I started to run. I ran past

the body of the lieutenant. I ran past the rabbit. I continued to run toward the border. Then a deer jumped out of the forest just ahead of me. There was a sudden loud explosion and the deer too was killed. I stopped and looked back at the major. He put his gun down and began to sob. He motioned to me to return. "I am sorry, little brother. My judgment is no good. I'm just trying to survive."

"So am I," I said.

In the end, we resigned ourselves to fate and returned to the darkness of the forest.

After seeing our companion die and realizing the hopelessness of making it out of Cambodia, we sat down and agreed we would go no further. I knelt and cried to the sky, "Why is this happening to me and my people?" I fell to the ground where the others were already lying, ready to accept death. I prayed to my parents, closed my eyes, and asked death to take me. I fell into a deep sleep.

I don't know how many minutes or hours or days I slept, but after a time I was awakened by someone whispering in my ear. At first I thought it was one of my companions, but everyone was asleep. A voice said to me, "Go this way." I could not see anyone and wondered if I was dreaming. But again and again I heard the voice. I asked myself, "Should I listen?" No, surely I was going mad. The voice, I told myself, was only the confusion of a mind on the edge of death. I tried to ignore the voice and go to sleep. But no sleep came, so I sat up and listened to the wind. Slowly, from far away and then growing closer, I heard music. I could not tell if it was coming out of the sky or out of my head. It was a song I had never heard before: a song for leading a procession or a parade.

As the music grew louder and louder, I began humming the melody. It filled me with energy. I jumped to my feet and woke everyone up. "Come on! Come on!" I shouted. "We are going this way!"

The men were so weak they could barely stand. Indeed I had to pull them up and lean them one by one against a tree. Then one would fall and I'd have to start again. I hummed the song that had come to me and drummed my chest. "Follow me! Follow me!" I shouted. And they did, without question, without protest, even the major.

I continued to hum the song and the men followed me in the direction the voice had indicated. We walked maybe three hundred meters, a long way for dying men to walk. I came to a pond of water. I splashed the water to my companions and urged them to follow me. I looked then to see a great tree filled with smooth pink and yellow fruit. It stood there, enormous, green, and majestic like a Chinese painting. I wondered for a moment whether or not it was real. I wondered why we had not seen it before. Standing next to it our human forms were diminished.

I climbed the tree and picked the fruit and threw it down to the men. They ate frantically and cried with happiness, knowing they would survive one more day. For a few minutes I stayed in the tree looking at them. Juice ran down their chins and onto their bodies. I smiled, thanked the tree, and joined the men in our feast.

The food gave us the strength to open our eyes and talk. One man asked me, "Little brother, what is the song that led us to this fruit?"

"I do not know," I told him.

This made us laugh—even though moments before we had been waiting for death. We hummed the song again. And whenever we were hungry the song returned to us. It provided us a rhythm to breathe by and gave us hope that we would live.

We lived in the forest for a while longer. And although I have other stories to tell, I want to say only one thing more about living in the forest: something about the meaning of that experience.

There are two Cambodian words for "forest." One is *"prey"* and the other is *"bali."* The word *"bali"* has different meanings too. It is the name of the monks' language and is used in their scripture; it also means something like "order or arrangement"; and lastly it means "bridge." For me this last meaning, bridge, is the most significant. The forest was a bridge between my former self and what I would become. In the forest I experienced life fully and witnessed its agony and its beauty. When I gave myself over to nature, I became not a man alone but a part of the mystery and order of life in such a way that my individual life no longer existed. And I knew that if I could attain the peace that comes with feeling at one with a worm, I could survive the darkness that was about to fall upon me.

In the end, though, hope alone could not sustain us. After all the fruit on the tree was gone, we walked for many days but could find nothing else to eat. As we walked, seemingly in circles, we came upon a watermelon farm. We hid behind a tree looking out at a whole field of watermelons. Watermelons are beautiful to a starving man: the difference between life and death.

A man guarded the field with a gun. I wanted to go and ask him for one of the melons, but I was afraid. The men and I sat debating with each other. Finally my hunger won and I walked over to the man. He stuck out his gun and said, "What is your function?" I did not know how to answer. Then I said, "They ordered me to cut trees but I got lost. Please, can you give me a watermelon?"

He looked at me. My hair and beard had grown long. After a moment, he said, "No. They belong to the Angkar," meaning the government.

"Might I have some water then?"

He agreed and took me to his hut. He gave me some water in a hollowed-out coconut shell. While I drank, he lit a cigarette and smoked it. He looked at me and asked, "Are you Mulatan or April 17?" I didn't know what he meant, so I avoided answering. I said, "I'm sorry. I really need to urinate." I slipped outside and hurried to the other men. "What does he mean, 'Mulatan or April 17'?" We guessed that he was trying to determine if I had supported the Khmer Rouge before the revolution.

I returned to the man and again he asked me if I was **75** Mulatan or April 17. "Mulatan, of course," I said.

The man came closer and touched my arm. "Okay," he said in a quiet voice. "You know Angkar's theory and proverbs. I'll give you a watermelon, but don't tell the April 17 people."

The man gave me a watermelon and I ate all of it. Then I asked him if I could bring the rest of my group so they too could have some watermelon. He agreed, so I brought them. Their eyes grew bright at the sight of the melon, and even before the guard could reach for a knife to cut it, the men broke it open and ate it with their fingers. When we had finished eating, the guard asked a question that made us think he was growing suspicious. We left as quickly as we could.

We stayed near that farm for ten days or so, and each night I stole a watermelon. We lived on nothing but watermelon until we began vomiting. I decided to return to the farm and look for something else to eat. I found a potato field. I dug up some potatoes, packed my pant legs full, and returned to the men.

We thought we might be able to continue to hide out and take food from the field, but one night when I went to the field, one of the guards heard me and asked the other, "What's that sound?" The other replied, "I think it's a pig," and he began shooting all around me. I crawled to the edge of the field and ran back into the forest. After that, the other men and I were afraid to go back. Anyway, I did not want to steal. I was not a pig but a man who, though dying of hunger, felt shame from having to steal.

The men and I talked about what we should do next. One of us said, "We cannot live in the forest anymore. It is just too difficult. If we stay any longer we will surely die." We all agreed. We had no choice but to surrender and go to a Khmer Rouge camp, though none of us wanted to surrender to the army that had tried to kill us. We hoped that since we had on the black clothes of the Khmer Rouge they would not kill us. We prepared ourselves, cutting our hair the best we could by spreading it on the stump of a tree and cutting it with a knife.

We walked until we came to a Khmer Rouge camp. A soldier was standing there alone. When he saw us, he stuck out his gun and asked, "Where are you from?"

I said, "We are from Pursat province."

The soldier's voice boomed, "We do not have provinces anymore! What district are you from?"

The men and I looked at each other. I wondered what had happened to our country and how I would answer his questions.

"We are from district eight," I said.

"District eight? There is no district eight! What cooperative do you belong to?" the soldier demanded.

"Uh . . . cooperative ten." Sweat began to pour down my face.

"Who is your cooperative leader?"

"His name is . . . Chhun Tha."

The soldier looked like he didn't believe me. He stuck the gun in my chest. "Why are you so far from your cooperative?"

"We were cutting trees and got lost."

"Where are your ax and saw?"

"They were too heavy to carry so we left them in the forest."

The soldier looked at our thin bodies. "How many days have you been lost?"

"Many days, maybe ten." In fact it had been seven or eight months.

"Ten days? How did you live?"

"We lived on leaves, that is all. Please, we are so hungry. Can we stay here in this cooperative?"

Another soldier appeared and asked me, "Do you know how to cut trees?"

"Oh, yes!" I lied. "I can cut very well."

"Is that true? Get up there and show me."

I climbed up and tried to saw the tree, but I was so thin and weak I could not. My arms shook. I became dizzy and fell to the ground. Another soldier watching this grabbed my arm. I looked into his eyes and begged him, "Please let me try again. It's just that I'm so hungry from being in the forest without food."

He hesitated for a moment but agreed and asked another soldier to give us some rice. The other men and I had not had rice in many months. We could hardly swallow it and nearly vomited.

As I ate, I watched the men in the distance cutting a log and recalled seeing how one of the prisoners who had lived with my family had used his saw. I remembered exactly the man's words and techniques. I saw everything in front of my eyes. After a few minutes the soldier said, "It is time to show me how well you can cut."

As I stood up, the other men whispered, "Be careful." I felt both afraid and confident. I began to saw that tree with a strength I had not felt in a year. The image of that prisoner cutting a log at my house stayed in front of my eyes. I cut that log fast and straight. Maybe the king-master had come to help me again.

When I had finished, we all looked at the soldier. "Okay, you can stay," he said.

I climbed down and the other men said to me, "It is because of you that we live." This would have made me happy, except that experience marked the beginning of my life under the oppression of the Khmer Rouge.

IV
Elegy

Many changes took place in Cambodia while we were in the forest. The horrible reality of what our country had become began to be revealed to us, not so much by words, but by silence. No one talked, no one laughed, no one sang. The only sounds were the sounds of work—hoes hitting the ground, saws cutting, and elephants dragging logs. The people were as silent and half-there as ghosts. In time we too became silent.

The first night in the cooperative we were sent to study. This consisted of sitting on the ground and listening to the rules of the Khmer Rouge society. In the dark, we could not see our teachers. We could only hear their voices. They told us not to gather in groups of more than two people and not to share ideas. We were expected, indeed pledged, to allow ourselves to be killed if we made a mistake.

The first step in our education was self-criticism: admitting our mistakes. That first night, a very thin older man said, "I apologize. I fell down while plowing today. I promise to work harder tomorrow."

In the view of the Khmer Rouge, the cities were the source of greed and selfishness. In the first days of the regime, all the cities and towns were emptied out. Everyone was moved to the countryside so that they could be reeducated in the ways of manual labor and cut off from the influence of Western culture.

All the people of Cambodia were assigned to coopera- tives. They labored in the countryside, growing rice, digging irrigation ditches, logging. The goal of this plan was national self-sufficiency—to end Cambodia's dependence on anyone else in the world. But it meant placing millions of people in places devoid of trees, digging dry soil, trying to bring it to life while attempting to forget the death around them. The people did not talk or smile or cry. Clothed in black, they worked silently, raising their hoes in the air and letting them fall to the earth with a thud.

In the cooperatives, families were separated. The elder people worked as cooks in huge kitchens and cared for the very young. The older children were taken away from their parents and put in what was called a school. In reality, I came to know, the school was a child labor camp and a place to indoctrinate the children in the ideas of the Khmer Rouge.

The whole population of Cambodia was divided into two categories. The "Mulatan" lived in areas the Khmer Rouge had controlled before 1975. They used this word that meant "base" because peasants were considered the foundation of the new society. Then there were the "April 17" people, people like myself who had not joined the Khmer Rouge before the revolution. The Mulatan were the leaders. It was easy to know who they were. They were not thin like the April 17 people and wore better clothes. Some had guns. They lacked fear and looked straight ahead as they walked, not down at the ground like the April 17 people.

We were instructed to devote ourselves to "Angkar Loeu," a term that means something like "Big Government." More than that, Angkar was devotion of yourself to something abstract and unknown, faceless but all-seeing. Our love for Angkar was meant to replace the love and devotion we held toward our parents, religion, and ideals. The Khmer Rouge tried in every way to break the mirrors that reflected the old Cambodia. To adopt any part of Western culture became a crime against the government: speaking foreign languages, wearing Western-style clothes, and singing any songs other than those of the Khmer Rouge. Everyone wore black clothes and rubber sandals.

Some of the changes in my life under the Khmer Rouge were tolerable and, in fact, better than my life in the forest. The absence of music, however, was hard for me. I missed music intensely. I missed the comfort it gave me and the memories it provided. Once early on in the cooperative, I began unconsciously to whistle a Western song. A man put his hand over my mouth and whispered, "They will kill you for knowing that song!" I felt my spirit sink.

Our days were filled with hard physical labor, but some time each day was given to reeducating us in the ways of the revolution. We never used books. Indeed many of the Khmer Rouge could not read. Instead we were told, "The rice field is your university," and, "Your hoe is your pen." We sat on the ground listening to the radio broadcast speeches of nameless Khmer Rouge leaders. We listened to them, over and over, so many times we could memorize them:

You and all our people must be constantly instructed and educated in collective, socialist ownership. You must eliminate the idea of private ownership.

In our new Cambodian society there are enemies in the form of various spy rings working for imperialism. Moreover, international reactionaries are still planted among us to carry out subversive activities against our revolution. These counterrevolutionary elements, which try to sabotage the revolution, are not to be regarded as being our people. They are to be regarded as enemies. . . . We must deal with them the same way we would with any enemy— that is, by separating, educating, and co-opting elements that can be won over . . . and neutralizing any reluctant elements.

There must have been many "reluctant elements" in Cambodia at that time because every night the soldiers took someone to kill. At first they did not kill in the light of day. The soldiers always took people at night and killed them in the animal world of the forest.

The soldiers were constantly looking for mistakes, indications of sabotage, enemies. They became more and more irrational. At first just the staff and military officers of the former government were killed. After a while, the definition of enemies expanded to include anyone with an education, anyone wearing glasses, then the families, even small children, of the enemy. People were killed for the smallest imperfection—asking a soldier a question, eating food other than that rationed to them, being late to work, anything at all. We used to say these men had pineapple eyes: hundreds of eyes looking for mistakes and reasons to kill.

One of the men I had been in the forest with made the fatal mistake of missing his family. He had not adjusted to living in the cooperative and became depressed. His depression made him careless, however, and he began to talk about missing his wife and children, missing his home in Phnom Penh, missing the feeling of being full. So one night the soldiers pulled him from his hammock and took him to the forest. We heard a single shot. They wanted to kill his idea of what society should be. That was how the soldiers were. They believed that in order to kill an idea you must kill the body.

I came to know all of this not at once but gradually over a number of weeks. When I realized what had happened, I cried to myself, "This is not Cambodia and these are not my people! Where is my Cambodia?" I could not comprehend.

Because it had been the primary goal of the Khmer Rouge to return Cambodia to its agrarian roots, most of the labor was targeted toward that end. Though our labor produced large quantities of rice, it was put in bags and loaded on a truck to go somewhere else. We were not told where it went and did not ask. We were only given a cup of rice each day, sometimes less. We all grew thin and small and weak.

To fully describe that period of my life, I must emphasize starvation and the preciousness of food. I once saw a half-smashed kernel of corn on the dusty road and picked it up and enjoyed it as if it were a meal. We began to measure food by the days it would sustain us. An orange could sustain me for a day. Receiving a potato was followed by a proclamation: "Three days of life!"

It was life, yes, but such a strange way of living. The Khmer Rouge tried to change our ideas about everything. After I was at the log camp for about a month, for instance, some of us were called to a meeting and told we were getting married. I looked at the girl standing beside me and thought: "How can I marry a woman I do not love and without our parents' permission?" But of course I had no choice. She looked no happier than I at the idea of marrying. I did not know the woman, though I had often seen her in the company of the cooperative leader. After we were gathered, the marriage ceremony began. We were ordered to lock hands and raise them and repeat after the leader something like, "I pledge allegiance to Angkar Loeu. I will obey the rules of the revolution and allow myself to be killed if I make a mistake." Then the ceremony was over and I was told I would have a new assignment in another cooperative.

This was nothing like the traditional way of marriage, which involves a ceremony lasting seven days. The traditional marriage between a boy and girl begins with their meeting and an indication to their parents that they love one another. The parents meet together three times. If they like each other and the birthdates of the girl and boy are compatible, an agreement is made for the boy to live with the girl's family for one year to be their servant. After the year is up, the parents meet again to share a feast of pig's head and wine. The girl's parents politely ask questions of the boy and his parents. "Have you ever stolen anything? Do you have any physical defects? Can you show us how you walk?" If all goes well, the boy says to the girl, "I need a path and I need the stairs to reach you." There is silence as the boy waits to hear the word "yes."

Rituals then take place on each of the seven days of marriage. Accompanying each ritual is a song. There is one ritual to cut the hair of the boy and girl. There is another to clean the girl's teeth to remove any trace of the dragon with poisonous teeth believed to reside within her. This is the elders' way of trying to make the boy and girl human. Music is played to remind them of their humanity and their sacred connection to each other.

When the boy finally goes to be with the girl, his family and a group of musicians go with him. He cannot walk in the opposite direction of any flowing body of water. When he arrives at the girl's house, she meets him at the bottom of the stairs and cleans his feet with perfumed water. After this final ceremony, the boy and girl are left alone in a room and the whole village dances until morning.

In 1976 there was still some freedom and people, if given permission, were allowed to move around the province. I asked if I could go find my younger brother Dararith.

I was granted permission to go and bring Dararith back with me if I found him. I went to the place where I had last seen him—at the temple where I had been herded with the other men to be killed. When I asked the people living in the village of Prey Slek where I might find my brother, they pointed to a cooperative nearby. I went there and saw many people, but no one was friendly. I asked one man if he knew my brother. He did not know my brother nor did anyone else. It seemed hopeless. By then it was almost sunset and people were returning from the fields and forest. Then I noticed a boy carrying firewood on his shoulder who appeared and disappeared in the brush. His walk was familiar. "Dararith!" I called. Though he had become, like me, much thinner and darker, I recognized him easily.

He looked at me and asked, "Are you my brother?"

"Of course I am your brother. Look at my face. Do you see Chamroeun? Do you see Reatrey?"

He threw the wood from his shoulder and we hugged each other for a long while and cried. I asked him, "Brother, have you seen Sthany?"

"Yes," he replied. "Sthany is living in another cooperative not far from here."

"Why don't the two of you live together?" I asked Dararith.

"Don't you know the Khmer Rouge? They want to divide brothers."

"Yes, brother, I know. But I've been given permission to bring you to my cooperative."

We talked to the leader of Dararith's cooperative and got permission for him to come live with me. Since there was a shortage of food in his cooperative, they agreed to let him leave. We then went to find Sthany in hopes he too could join us. We found him easily at another cooperative nearby. Sthany cried when he saw us. The three of us embraced. We asked each other: "What about mother?" "What happened to Chamroeun?" "Can we go home to look for them?" But none of us had the answers.

For me there was a brief moment of happiness being back with my brothers again. But Sthany did not live with us for long. One day he came to me shyly and explained that he wanted to follow his girlfriend who, because she was half-Chinese, was being allowed to go to Vietnam. Sthany had never had much success with girls, blaming his thick, curly hair for his unattractiveness. I said to him, "Sthany, I'm surprised. You have never been in love before. Not only that but love is a dangerous thing under the Khmer Rouge." He agreed, but he wanted to return to the girl and so he left. Although we did not want him to go away, how could we deny him the pleasure of love? We learned later that the Khmer Rouge would not allow him to go. They pushed him off the boat. He disappeared after that.

Dararith and I continued to live in the same area. He stayed at the boarding school for children, studying and tending the animals. Sometimes he came to sleep with me. He came most often when he thought about our parents. He would cry and whisper, "I miss Mother and Father." I tried to teach him to hold in his tears. Dararith came to me when he was hungry. It hurt me to see his swollen stomach and I gave him whatever food I had.

One day I returned from the fields to find Dararith not tending the cows as he should but sitting on some stairs crying. His leg was swollen and bleeding. "Brother, what happened?" I asked.

"The leader of my group hit me."

"Why did he hit you?" I asked.

"I don't know. Maybe because the cows ate some of the rice seedlings."

Anger rushed through my body. I took Dararith and went to the group leader and asked him why he had hit my brother. "You don't need to know about that," he said.

"Is this the rule of our new Cambodia, to hit children for things that are not their fault?" I asked him.

We were standing in the rice field. The leader took a stick and tried to hit me. I took it away from him and hit him on the leg. I asked him, "Do you feel that pain in your leg? Now you feel the pain of my brother." I kicked the man into the mud. I knew I could be killed for doing such a thing, but in compassion for my brother I forgot about my own life.

The leader was furious and went to tell his supervisor of my mistake. Later that evening, I decided I had to find out what would happen to me. As I walked past a group of leaders all dressed in black and squatting on the ground under a tree, I heard them say my name. I hid in a mango tree and listened to them. They were discussing what had happened. If they decided to kill me, I planned to run away. Two of the section leaders, Mr. Sann and Mr. Aung, defended me by saying I was a hard worker and had never caused any trouble. At last I heard the big leader say, "Let him live."

The Khmer Rouge decided to separate me from my brother again, however, and I was given a new assignment in another place. That assignment was digging irrigation ditches. This work was very difficult because the ground was so hard—really rock, not much dirt at all. The Khmer Rouge did not think of that. They only knew that they wanted to make every part of Cambodia a rice field and water would make it possible.

The importance of water was in the minds of the Khmer Rouge just as it had been in the minds of Cambodians for hundreds of years, since the time of King Indravarman. This king started irrigation projects to tap the power of water and created a mythological home of the gods called Angkor Wat. Angkor Wat is the largest religious building in the world, but it is also an extensive waterworks project. It is surrounded by water and to reach the temple one must cross a two-hundred-meter-long bridge. The water brought life to the rice fields surrounding the temple. With four harvests a year, the people grew strong and the Cambodian empire flourished. That was the golden age of the Cambodian people.

The Khmer Rouge tried to return our country to that

greatness. The subject of canals was always in the speeches of the leaders. They said things like, "We will no longer be dependent on nature," and, "The canals are our veins."

My life in those days was the canal. In a sense you could say I was living in the veins of the Khmer Rouge. I worked in the ditch all day and slept in it at night on the long flat basket that I used to carry the dirt and rocks. I laid the basket over the trickle of water running through the canal and curled my body on top of it. It was cold and damp in there, like a grave. Living in the canal, my skin came to have the scent of the earth. Once more I felt I was part of nature. Each morning I would pound my chest to expel the water I had breathed in during the night.

Once while sleeping in the ditch I had a dream about fighting off an enemy and I fell in the water. I awoke and took my clothes off to wring them out and put them back on. I shivered and thought of the misery of my life. Even sleep offered no refuge.

By that time I had lived under the Khmer Rouge for three or four months. It had been more than a year since I had seen my parents and my other brothers and my sister Raksmey. And although I tried not to think of them, the memories and the longing were hard to stop.

One night, without thinking, I began to whistle a song that my family used to play. It was a song about a boy riding away on a horse while sadly saying good-bye to a girl he loved. Whenever anyone in my family went away—when we returned to school after a holiday, for example—my mother would say, "Daran, go get your brothers and play that song for me." It was this song I was whistling when I was interrupted by a soldier looking down at me in the ditch. "Get out of the ditch!" he demanded. I had a sick feeling as I realized what I had done. I climbed out and stood before the soldier. He looked at me and said, "Go to the forest."

I walked to the trees and saw some other soldiers there. They were told what I had done. They said, "This is your mistake. You know we do not allow capitalist songs."

"Yes," I lied. "But the song I was whistling is a Communist song."

One of them replied, "I am a musician and I've never heard that song before."

"You are a musician? What instrument do you play?" I asked, knowing I was not allowed to ask questions but sensing he was proud of his musical abilities.

"I play the guitar and the pianica."

One of the soldiers looked at him and said, "I've never seen a pianica before. What does it look like?"

"I have one here in my pack," the first soldier said, reaching for it. It was a long, flat instrument, like a flute with a keyboard along the top. He motioned to me. "Do you know how to play this?"

"Maybe," I said.

I didn't really know how it was played, but I guessed it was like an accordion. The soldier offered it to me and I took it and began to play a popular Communist song. The men listened. After I finished, there was silence. Then one of them told me to sit down while they had a discussion. The men walked further into the forest, about fifteen meters away, and talked. I could not hear them, and because it was dark I could only see the outlines of their bodies and their shadows when they moved. I was afraid they would kill me and I was tempted to run away, but I didn't.

Then one of them called to me. I walked cautiously toward them. "Come quickly!" he demanded. I walked faster and saw their guns propped against a tree. I realized then that they weren't going to kill me after all. The light from a kerosene lantern revealed their faces. Before, their faces had been like my enemy, but they weren't my enemy any longer.

One of them said to me, "What you have done is against

the rules if that song is indeed a capitalist song. We don't know, so we won't kill you. Just don't whistle it anymore."

I returned to the ditch, lay down, and allowed my heart to quiet. After that I tried never again to whistle. But at times my mind would drift, my lips pursed, and a song emerged without any thought or intention from me.

After that incident, the soldiers sometimes gathered around my underground bed to request a song, which I played on the soldier's pianica. The sound of music traveled, and once a girl of seventeen or eighteen came and called down to me, "When I hear you play, it reminds me of my father. Could you come sometime and play for me and some of the others?"

One of the soldiers heard what she had said. He grabbed her shirt and led her away. I heard him say, "Your father? You miss your father? Devotion to your parents is just a capitalist notion." I saw him push her into the ditch and then I hid further down in the ditch and heard him rape her. After a half hour or so he took her out of the ditch. I heard her call out from the forest in a small voice, "No, no." A pain grew in my throat and stomach and head. I listened, all the while trying to stop myself from thinking about what was happening. My desire to help her was in conflict with my concern for my own life. I talked to myself and repeated the Buddhist proverb: "That being present, this becomes. Being not present, this does not become." When it got quiet, I slept for a while but kept waking up. In the morning someone said he had found the girl's dead body against a tree. And though I did not want to be present, I was. I was present within myself and with her.

I never grew used to the killing. It stirred strong feelings in me. Each time I knew someone was killed, I would talk to myself and say: "Daran, think of yourself. Do not feel the pain of anyone else or you will die too." I tried to suppress my emotions, my feelings of compassion for the victims, and my hatred for those who preyed upon them.

Living in the canal, in the rock of the earth, reminded me of something with my father. When I was about nine years old, my father wanted to build a fence around our house with a stone entrance. He called my brothers Chamroeun, Bunly, and me to come help him. He was getting old and wanted to pass on his knowledge to us.

My father had gathered rocks of various sizes and shapes and cement to join them together. My father was a man who thought deeply even when doing manual labor. Before we began to work he said, "Wouldn't it be good if each of these rocks were perfectly square? Then our work would be easy. But that is not the way nature made them. Nor do we have the tools to make them square. These rocks have a thousand shapes, like a thousand faces, like a thousand ideas. They are like a puzzle, incomplete, and not strong on their own. But, you see, if we accept them as they are and put them all together and bind them with cement, they will be good and strong. In the end, when we are finished, we will have the square. When you see this gate, think of that."

When the work was completed, my father carved his initials, "K. B.," in the rock so they could be seen from far away. We returned to our house proud of our work and full of our father's words.

Though I couldn't see how the terrible faces and ideas of the Khmer Rouge fit into the whole of life, I still believed in my father's wisdom.

I lived in the veins of the Khmer Rouge for a few more months. One day during this time, I discovered a clever way of digging quickly by using leverage. The leaders got very excited and said to me, "You are the son of Angkar! We can give you a reward. Would you like a bag of tobacco?" I told them, "No, I don't need any tobacco. I would like to see my brother again." My request was denied. I was told I would have another assignment in a place called Khbal Boeung.

My assignment at Khbal Boeung was to supervise twenty children in the production of fertilizer. We collected metal boxes of human waste, poured ashes on it, and mixed it with dirt. We had to use our bare hands or feet because there weren't enough shovels. We shaped the mixture into bricks and put them in the sun to dry. Then the bricks were transported to the fields to fertilize the crops. I was sickened by the smell, but it was my responsibility to keep the children from vomiting as they worked. I told them, "Take a deep breath so you are full of the smell and cannot smell anymore." I tried to make a game of it and said, "If you do it you'll be a hero!" They did not look like heroes. Their stomachs were swollen and their faces were ugly with hopelessness.

The children of Cambodia under the Khmer Rouge were not really children at all. Some were recruited as spies. Some had seen their parents killed and were scared all the time. Because of their young age, they had not learned how to deal with life's difficulties. They still lived close to their childhood fears and could not escape them, not in their sleep, not anytime. I sympathized with the children. They were so innocent and small. They needed milk and fruit to eat. The Khmer Rouge taught them not to love their parents or miss them. Why they would do this, I still do not know. The children were told such things as: "Your hair belongs to your head." "No one can die for you." "Don't rely on your parents, rely on Angkar."

Sometimes the children would be reminded of their parents and would cry and cry. Sometimes they would kick the ground and scream, "I want my mom!" But when the soldiers came close, they stopped right away. They stood silent, sucking on their fingers. Sometimes they wanted to run away to look for their parents. I did what I could to console them. I would tell them, "Try to forget, try to forget. Just work and when you finish we will dance and sing songs of expectation." At break time I'd take them to put their feet in the river.

Khbal Boeung was next to a large lake covered by water hyacinths. Everyone was afraid of the lake because of a traditional story of what happened long ago. At one time there had been a temple near the lake where several monks lived. One day one of the monks found a crocodile egg, and he kept it until the crocodile hatched. The baby crocodile grew and came to love the monk very much and was his servant. The monk rode on the crocodile's back across the lake. Then one day some crocodiles from another area came to the lake. A big fight began and the crocodile said to his owner, "Let me swallow you to protect you from the other crocodiles." The monk agreed. But this did not save the monk or the crocodile. The crocodiles destroyed the temple and at last it sank into the lake.

When the Khmer Rouge arrived, statues of crocodiles were still there but the soldiers smashed them. This upset the people because they believed that if the statues were broken the people would soon die. I knew of this story and the bad spirits that were supposed to live in the lake. But my curiosity became stronger than my fear and one day I pushed back the reeds beside the water to have a look. What I saw was great numbers of fish! I thought of these fish for many days and decided I'd try to catch some to eat.

During the night I secretly made a trap and placed it where the lake ran into a river. Before dawn I went to check the trap and found many fish. I ate the fish and felt happy and full for the first time in months, but I knew I was doing something against Angkar. Fearing the consequences of my actions, I took a basket of fish to the section leader, Mr. Veng, and whispered to him, "I have a lot of fish. I give them to Angkar now." I laid the fish in front of him.

"Where did you get them?" he asked me.

"I made a trap and caught them in the lake."

"In the lake?"

"Yes, there are many fish there."

Mr. Veng looked at me with a long face. "Oh, you are not allowed to think about the personal. Everything, including these fish, belongs to Angkar."

"Yes, I know," I replied. "That is why I brought them to you. I can share them with everyone. Please come with me to get some more."

After some thought, Mr. Veng agreed and we went to collect the trap. It was so full of fish it took Mr. Veng and me and his wife to lift it from the water. We took it to the kitchen and then called the people to come and eat.

Everyone was pleased. They asked me where I had found so many fish. I told them I had taken the fish from the lake. They were surprised and a little frightened of eating fish from a lake filled with crocodiles and bad spirits. I reassured them: "I looked myself and saw not one crocodile. Come with me, and I'll pull back the reeds and you can look for yourself."

Some of them followed. I said, "If you overcome your fear, the lake will give you life, not death." After that, one, then two, then three men went to fish at the lake. I watched from the shore as they grew braver and waded into the water. Others joined in. Soon all the men of the village were taking torches to the lake at night to attract fish. There were many fish—so many, in fact, they jumped from the water and hit people's faces. For hungry people, it was a wonderful thing to have fish jumping into their nets. I watched with delight.

This went on for a week or two. The people's fear of the lake disappeared and their stomachs grew full. I knew Angkar would become concerned at the strength people gained from eating so much fish. It was not long before the leader of the camp called Mr. Veng and asked him who had been first to fish the lake. Mr. Veng told him my name. Mr. Veng apologized to me, saying, "I am sorry, Daran, I cannot lie to Angkar. If I do, they will take me to the forest and kill me."

I hardly slept that night, expecting to be visited by the soldiers. But morning came and I looked at my rising chest and I said to myself, "I'm alive!" This gave me hope.

While I was still lying down, Mr. Veng came to tell me that the leader wanted to see me. "What can I say?" I asked. Mr. Veng only shook his head. My fear returned.

I went to the leader, whose name was Mr. Nhek. He said, "Why did you do something against Angkar rule?"

"I only wanted to make the people stronger so they could work harder for Angkar."

"But Angkar says, 'Eat a little, work a lot.'"

I changed my voice. "Yes, we can do that if you wish. But could I suggest something to you?"

"What?" he asked.

"May I suggest you allow people some small happiness? Could you allow them to take just a little fish? The people will follow you if they believe you care for them."

He thought for a few minutes without giving me any indication of what he was thinking. The silence made me very uncomfortable. I said, "You know people can eat the reeds too and not eat so much rice. Then there will be more rice for Angkar." There was more silence.

I finally asked him, "Should I go somewhere now?" I was expecting him to order me to the forest.

"Yes," he said. "Go back to your hut."

I left Mr. Nhek then. Outside many people were waiting to learn of my fate. They were surprised that nothing had happened to me. A man said to me, "Nobody can talk to Angkar like you." A small, old woman took my hand and said, "Oh, grandson, I wish you a long life."

Hundreds of years ago Cambodian people made an oath to the king which is inscribed in stone: "If all of us here in person do not keep this oath with regard to His Majesty—may he reign long—we ask that he inflict on us royal punishment of all sorts."

This subordination to the king was still present in the minds of Cambodians in the 1960s when Prince Sihanouk regularly had his men kidnap and kill outspoken intellectuals. Sihanouk was responsible for the deaths of many and the disappearance of thousands more. Seven million people knew this, but no one protested because they believed Sihanouk was good. In the Cambodian mind, it was reasonable and simple to understand that if you said something bad about the king you would be punished.

So even in the Khmer Rouge regime no one protested about the lack of human rights. We quickly learned that if we protested we could be grabbed by the ear and shot in the head. There was no such thing as justice, no policemen, no human rights, no judges. And if we had been allowed to ask for anything, we would not have asked for justice. We would have asked for food.

Cambodian proverbs are often about the helplessness of the individual and one's need to accept powerful forces as they are. As children, all Cambodians are taught the "Reamker," which is a long book of epic poetry and prose carved into the walls of the ancient temple at Angkor Wat. It speaks of the balance and constant struggle between good and evil. It teaches that both good and evil must survive in order to define each other. This too was in the minds of Cambodians.

Although I was too scared to protest against the evil I saw under the Khmer Rouge, a rage burned within me. During that time, I reminded myself of my father's teachings. After a boy spit on Chamroeun, my father tried to calm Chamroeun's anger. He said, "If they hit you, you will sleep well. But if you hit them, you will not sleep well."

I stayed in Khbal Boeung cooperative for a few months and then was sent back to the logging cooperative. And there something magical happened to me. One day as I worked, I was thinking about the accordion my father had given me. Just then I saw a soldier ride by on a bicycle. On the back of his bicycle was an accordion. Had I imagined it? I thought about it for a long while. Was it a trick of the gods? Was it a ghost accordion?

Weeks later as I walked alone in the forest, I again saw an accordion. It was an old, red accordion and it lay before me on the stump of a tree. Was it real or only wishful thinking? Why was it there? Where had it come from? I wanted to play it and looked around to see if anyone was watching. I did not see anyone, so I put down my saw and delicately picked up the accordion as if it were a newborn baby. Quietly I played a few notes. My heart pounded as it had the first time I played it when I was eight years old.

Without warning, from nowhere, a soldier appeared and said, "Do you know how to play that?"

My heart hammered in my chest. I looked at him in silence, not knowing what to say. I thought to myself, if I tell the truth he might know I am educated and kill me. But maybe it would please him if I can play. I could not read his face. Was he tricking me? Would my playing bring me a tiger or a deer? My mind sifted through all these questions while my fingers and my heart cried out for me to play. I had been starved for music. I needed its comfort. I said, "Yes, I can play a little."

The soldier smiled, then sat on the stump and ordered me to play for him. I played a popular Communist song. I cannot describe the feeling I had as the first note hit the air! It was such a beautiful and powerful thing that it made me forget all my misery. The soldier enjoyed it. He lit a cigarette, listened, and tapped his foot to the sound. I knew then he would not kill me.

That was the beginning of a bit of friendliness between us. He was not so strict with me. I can't say whether he liked me or he liked my music. I always waited impatiently for the moment when he said, "Play a song for me." I am reminded of the Cambodian term "to like." The word is *"chuelchet,"* and translated it means "into the heart."

Once when I was playing a song for this soldier, another soldier overheard us. He was a truck driver who brought supplies to the camp. He usually returned to town in the evening, but one time a flooded river blocked his path and he came back to the camp. He heard me playing, sat down to listen, and decided to stay the night. After that he often stayed the night so he could hear my music.

This soldier would often request a song called "Red Silk Scarf." This is a song about the Cambodian custom of a boy wearing a silk scarf until it is permeated with his scent. Then he gives it to a girl for her to wear so she will remember him after they are separated. She wears it every time her memory of him starts to fade. This song is usually played on the Cambodian violin. The singer wails in loneliness, and all who listen are filled with compassion and sadness. The song was a favorite of my father's.

One time after I had played especially well, the man asked me if I'd like to keep the accordion as my own. I felt I should refuse. "No, that is not necessary for me," I said.

"You are correct. That is not necessary for you. But maybe Angkar wants to hear music sometimes."

"In that case I would be happy to receive it," I told him.

When the soldier gave me the accordion a few days later, I was ecstatic. It was like a gift from Buddha, though it came from a man who was my enemy. It had the words "Made in Italy" on it. I wondered how it had made its way to Cambodia, and I speculated about who its owner had been. It was old, faded, and rusty. It had a hole in the bellows and seven or eight keys were broken so its sound was a little strange. But it was nonetheless an accordion and I loved it.

I played my accordion for this soldier many times, and he secretly rewarded me with cans of kerosene for my lantern and extra food. I shared this with the others and we sat together in a circle, enjoying the light of the lantern and the extra nourishment that were gifts in exchange for my music. These things kept us all alive a little longer. Everyone spoke of me with praise and brought me as close to bliss as one could get in the dark time of the Khmer Rouge.

One day while playing for this soldier one of the section leaders, Mr. Chhoeun, heard my accordion's voice. He took me aside and quietly said, "I can play the mandolin. Why don't we play together away from the others?"

I agreed. Each day after our work was finished, we would cross the field and ford a small stream and begin to play together under the shade of a tree. There was a bit of joy in that time. I felt like a child again playing music with my brothers. Playing music together made us brothers. Mr. Chhoeun and I played together often. Because he was Mula-tan, he had the freedom to play. In time our playing was no longer a secret. People began to gather around us just to stand and listen. I thought to myself, "Why do people come to listen to this music when they barely have strength to stand? Why don't they go looking for a potato or a few leaves to eat?" And I wondered, why did I not do the same? It seemed I was finding my strength in the music. I came to understand that playing music recreated everything that I had lost: my mother, my farm, my peace, the closeness of brothers. These things were sometimes more important than food to sustaining me. So I played my music and survived one more day.

Cambodia has forty-four indigenous instruments made of wood, bamboo, shell, ivory, snakeskin, or buffalo horn. We have created flutelike instruments that heal the sick, instruments played solo during poetry readings, and instruments played only at royal ceremonies. Some instruments were created by children tending cattle; others are believed to attract supernatural beings. We have drums that are considered sacred. Whenever an instrument is made, prayers are offered to ensure the best sound.

No one knows how many songs Cambodians have created. They are too numerous—as numerous, in fact, as there are human actions. There is music to remind us of every emotion and all that is sacred to us. Music reminds us of our long history, the sacrifice of our parents, our desire for love, our commonality as human beings. And the power of music followed us into the Khmer Rouge regime.

Mr. Chhoeun came to love me as a brother. He did kind things for me. One day he gave me a bag of rice bran which I turned into little cakes to share with the others. One of these people was a man who lived near me. He was a quiet man, a little old. He had arrived late in our cooperative from the east with trainloads of other people. They were sent to us because they lived near the Vietnam border and the Khmer Rouge did not want them to escape into that country. When they arrived they still had colorful clothes, perfume, and jewelry. But after ten days or so, they were wearing black clothes and rubber sandals and looked just like us.

One night I walked past this man's hut and saw him sitting in the dark. I went and took a torch for him. As I approached his hut, he called out, "Who is there?"

"It is me, Daran," I said.

"Who is Daran?"

"I am the one who plays the accordion. I have some bran cakes for you."

The man said softly, "Brother, come sit here beside me."

The man took a few bites of the bran cakes and began to talk. He said he had wanted to talk before but had been too scared. He told me he was a musician, a mandolin player and a composer. The man said, "I do not mind letting go of my personal possessions, but I can't let go of my music. I have kept my mandolin and some written music. Come with me and I will show you."

Then a strange thing happened. He took me behind his hut and dug in the ground where he had hidden some sheet music. He spoke of the songs and the composer. And then he told me the composer's name. It was my brother's name!

I began to cry and the man asked me why. I told him, "Chamroeun is my brother. My real blood brother." The man was very surprised and said, "This is a big country and this piece of paper is so small. How could it have found its way to you?" This man was the famous Svay Sam Oeur, the finest mandolin player in Cambodia.

Weeks went by and word reached the cooperative leader that I was able to play music. This leader was a woman named Miss Khon. She had replaced Mr. Nhek when he was taken away to be killed because the Khmer Rouge believed he had been disloyal.

One day Miss Khon came to see me while I was cutting a log. She asked me, "Are you the one who plays the strange instrument?"

"Yes," I said.

"Then I order you to play!" she said in a stern voice.

I was so scared I jumped down and ran to get my accordion and find Mr. Chhoeun. I looked for him everywhere and finally I saw him and exclaimed, "We must play music right away for Angkar!"

We returned to the leader, who stood waiting. Armed bodyguards were on either side of her. She did not have a gun. She did not need one. If she wanted someone to die, she just used her voice. I was nervous and my arms were shaking from having cut logs all day. I wondered how well I'd be able to play. Miss Khon asked, "What do you call that instrument?"

"It is called an accordion," I said.

"Is that a Cambodian word?" she asked.

"No," was all I said.

"Did you make that instrument yourself?" she asked.

"No," is all I said again.

I grew more tense. I waited for Mr. Chhoeun to tune his mandolin. Miss Khon grew impatient and yelled at us to hurry. When we were ready to start, I asked the leader what song she wanted. She said she wanted to hear a song called "The Children Love Angkar without Limit." I played and she listened while staring at the accordion. Then she sat down and asked us for another song. I don't remember what that song was. Then she requested a third song, "The Children Work on the Railroad."

The last song she asked for was a song about how the capitalists killed the Khmer Rouge by hanging them from trees. The Khmer Rouge loved this song because it filled them with emotion and gave them a taste for revenge. As the leader sang along with the music, it appeared some distant emotions were flooding back to her. I recognized the look because I had seen the same expression on my mother's face. Tears formed at the edges of her eyes. I pretended not to notice. After we had finished she stood up, put her hand on my shoulder, and said: "I want you to come play for me at my house." Many times after that she ordered me to play.

Once when I went to the leader's house, she asked me if I would like a bag of jewelry in exchange for my music. But what good was jewelry to me? I said, "Thank you so much. But may I have some sugar or oranges instead?"

She told me, "Yes, take what you like."

I took the sugar and oranges and left her house running to share them with the others. Giving another person an orange was not just giving them an orange. It was giving them a day of life. So you can imagine my pleasure when I stood before my friends offering them an orange in the palm of one hand and a piece of sugar in the other.

One day I was summoned to Miss Khon's house. She requested many songs and I played for hours. When I stopped she said, "I am thinking of organizing a musician's group to play for the people. What do you think?" I told her I thought music would be very good for the people. It would make them happier and stronger. She said, "Yes, maybe."

Not long after that Miss Khon called a meeting. She asked

the crowd, "Who here can play music?" No one wanted to identify themselves. She spoke again. "I assure you, you can tell me without any ill effect. And even if you do not tell me, it is easy for me to find out." Then a man I came to know as Mr. Ly came close to my ear and said, "Are you Mulatan or April 17?" I told him I was April 17. He told me he knew I played music for the cooperative leader. He asked me in a quiet voice, "Can I tell the truth and say I can play the guitar?" I told him, "Yes, I think you can say you are able to play a little. But don't say anything more."

After more assurances from Miss Khon, Mr. Ly raised his hand, and then another person, and then two more raised their hands. And that was the beginning of our musicians' group.

This leads me to an important part of my story: living with the other musicians at a place called Kraing Chapay. *"Kraing"* means encyclopedia and *"Chapay"* means guitar. These words, Kraing Chapay, evoke a flood of memories in my mind—memories of a deep connection to other people and a realization of the sacrifices people can make for each other during the darkest periods of life.

The day after Miss Khon called the meeting, the Khmer Rouge leaders rounded up all the musicians and told us to walk to the forest. We were instructed not to bring anything except our musical instruments. The other musicians and I walked while the soldiers rode their bicycles. Thinking that maybe they were taking us out to kill us, we walked with our eyes wide open and our hearts beating fast. But we arrived in Kraing Chapay safely and were instructed to convert the forest into a farm. They told us we were not to go outside the area nor could anyone visit us.

We arrived in the forest with only each other and our instruments. We had none of the things we needed to start a farm. We wondered how we would survive. The first night we sat around a fire and talked. I thought maybe the cooperative leader had tricked me. We concluded that the Khmer Rouge wanted to keep us separate from the people so they could control the power of our music and test our value as laborers. Our chances for survival did not seem promising.

I tried to relieve our worry by joking: "Maybe the Khmer Rouge want us to use our instruments to dig the ground. Would it make Angkar happy if I were to break up my accordion and turn it into a shovel?" Then my companions joined in.

"Right! I can take my guitar and make a hoe!"

"And I can make a hole in the ground with my violin!"

"And I can carry water in my drum!"

Despite being hungry and worried, we laughed and decided to play a song together. Our song turned into a concert. We played and let our spirits release us from our troubles.

The sound traveled. After a while children came out of the forest from nearby villages to listen to our music. We asked them, "Do you have a hoe or some seeds?" The next day they brought us the things we needed. And that is how we came to use our musical instruments to make a garden of cucumbers, melons, and potatoes.

I lived in Kraing Chapay with seven other musicians: Ly, a guitar player; Phan, Chhit, and Mao, who all played the Cambodian violin; Chhoeun, who played the mandolin; Rom, a drummer; and the most famous and talented among us, Svay Sam Oeur, the composer and mandolin player. Together we built a house consisting simply of a raised floor, a roof, and some posts along the sides. On the beams above us, we hung our instruments. It was a simple life of solitude. Our days consisted of working in the garden. At night we played music. It was better than living in the cooperative.

Life was not always peaceful. As musicians, we knew we were enemies of the Khmer Rouge. We realized we must try to protect each other. So we devised a system to warn each other during the night if we sensed something or someone approaching. The first person near the entrance would pinch the next person and he would pinch the next person and so on until the last person was pinched. That person would then pinch the person who had just pinched him and so on. During the day we tried not to think about frightening things at all. We worked in the fields and comforted ourselves with music. But in Kraing Chapay, as in all of Cambodia, the night brought fear and we sought each other for comfort.

I had a special bond with these men that I did not experience with my companions in the forest. I can only attribute this to the fact that we were all musicians and communicated with each other through our music as I had with my brother Chamroeun. I loved these men and they loved me, though at times there was conflict. I once had a disagreement with Mr. Ly. We had all decided to play music together, but Mr. Ly was absent. I went to him and said, "Brother, we want to play music. Won't you join us?"

"No," he replied. "It is against Angkar to play music for our own pleasure."

"Do you really believe that?" I asked him.

"Yes."

"But the children have come to hear us play. What about their desire for happiness?" I asked.

"That is not as important as work."

"Please, brother Ly. It's beautiful when we play together. If your guitar voice is not there, it's not the same. We will feel a gap."

He looked at me with a cold face. "My guitar string is broken."

"Yes? When did that happen?"

"Five minutes ago."

I didn't believe him. "Can you show me which of these strings is broken?" I asked. He said nothing. I left Ly there. I felt angry, but also sympathetic. I knew he was fighting the depression all of us felt.

One day I was working in the field with Mr. Ly. He

stopped and said, "I am so tired. Can you dig for me and I'll just sit there in the shadow of the tree and sing and tell you stories?"

"Yes, brother," I said.

Mr. Ly lay down, closed his eyes, and let his mind drift away. He began: "I am sitting under a tree, I am leaning against a tree, because I want to share a story with Daran. Daran is digging a hole for me so I can rest. The Khmer Rouge tell me I cannot think of my family, but I do. I think of my wife and my children and my parents and our life before in peace."

I stopped him. "If you talk about your family, I'll think of mine and I won't be able to work anymore." Mr. Ly began to cry. I went over to him and knelt down and put my hand on his shoulder. I reminded him the Khmer Rouge do not allow us to talk of our families. "Talk about something else," I said.

After some silence, Mr. Ly told me a funny story of going to the countryside to enter a cow riding contest. I laughed and told him, "Laugh and smile right now." He did. He smiled and laughed without any reason. Then he began to sing a forbidden song. When we saw the Khmer Rouge coming, I stopped him and said, "Change the words to express your love of Angkar." But I think it was too late. The soldiers saw him resting and singing. And that was his mistake.

It is partly because of Mr. Ly's death that I am now alive. It is a painful memory which returns to me whenever I hear a guitar. It happened on a day we were all working in the fields. I heard a woman's voice calling my name and I returned to the house to find the woman I was married to. We had not seen each other in nearly two years. She had been the mistress of one of the Khmer Rouge leaders. Consequently, she was given adequate food and was strong and not too thin. "What are you doing here?" I asked her.

"I heard you were here and I missed you."

We were like strangers and I became confused. She came

close to me and said she wanted to make love. "I cannot do that," I told her. Not only was I very thin and weakened, but I did not love her. She began to cry and plead with me. "Why?" I asked her over and over. She didn't reply. Instead she led me to the forest and kissed me and soon I was able to make love to her. But she was acting strange, crying all the while and pulling her scarf over her face. I don't know why she wanted to make love and I don't know why she cried. I didn't ask her. Neither of us said anything.

After that she took some water from the hut and hid behind a nearby hill and urinated. Then she said good-bye and I returned to the other men. They asked me what had happened and I told them. Some of them chuckled and some looked at me with long faces. "Be careful, Daran," they said. Thirty or forty minutes later a soldier coming to our hut to check on us saw where the woman had urinated. He asked in a loud voice, "Has there been a girl here?" All of us denied anyone had been there.

The soldier said, "No? There was a girl here not one hour ago! I have evidence." The soldier led us to the place where she had urinated and pointed out the position of the foot-prints. "I want the person who met her to speak up!" he said. Still no one said anything. The soldier stared at each of our faces, then left without saying anything more.

By that time it was growing dark. We ate in silence and lay down to sleep. I was so scared I slept only a short while. I lay on my side and pressed my ear to the floor. I felt movement but heard nothing. I began to grow scared. I pinched the man next to me but he was sleeping so soundly he did not feel it. I tried again but still he did not wake up. Slowly I raised my head to see if everyone was there. I counted only six men. Then I saw the empty place on the floor below Mr. Ly's guitar.

From the forest I began to hear faint cries. I sat stiff. I felt sick to my stomach at the thought of what might be happening. I wanted to escape my present life. What could I do? I could not run. I could not do anything. Finally, near dawn, I forced myself into a forgetful sleep. Later the other men woke me up. They gathered around me and laughed. "Oh, Daran, you make love with a woman once in two years and now you're exhausted!" I did not laugh. I did not say anything. I went to work in the garden.

Then one of the other men asked, "Where is Ly? Did he say he was going somewhere?" Still I did not say anything. I was too upset and afraid. I looked at my hoe hitting the ground over and over again. Tears welled up in my eyes. Then it was midday and each of us did something in preparation for our meal. One person dug up some potatoes, another poured some water. I went into the forest to find some firewood. It was there I saw Ly's lifeless body. He had been beaten to death. I returned to the men and told them what I had seen. Someone said, "Let's not talk. Let's just eat and work, that's all." But I could not eat.

The sound of a lone guitar still carries Mr. Ly's voice to me. I sometimes think it is a sound of forgiveness but sometimes I do not know. This part of my story makes me feel deeply ashamed. But it is true and I must say: Mr. Ly died for me and I survived one more day.

After that, the soldiers watched us more closely. Every day they counted the number of ripe fruit and vegetables. One day the other men and I noticed a watermelon was missing. It was a big one and it was obvious it had been picked. There was no sign that an animal had taken it. When the soldiers came we didn't say anything. We only watched each other through the corners of our eyes. When the two soldiers noticed the watermelon was missing they ordered us to assemble. They were very angry. One soldier emphasized his words by kicking the house post while he talked. The other continually picked up his rifle and put it down again loudly.

The two soldiers told us we would have one week to decide who had taken the watermelon. If no one confessed, they would kill us all.

After the soldiers left, we discussed what we would do. None of us had taken the watermelon. We lived so close together we would have known who had eaten it. Svay was very depressed at that time. He said, "I want to say I took the watermelon. I didn't really take it. But if I say I did, you will be saved. I don't mind if I die."

Someone said, "No! We need to stay united to be strong. I hate the Khmer Rouge. Look how they have tried to divide everyone, make us all enemies of one another!"

Svay continued to talk about his desire for death.

"No, Svay," I said. "Don't you see they want to kill all the artists and musicians of Cambodia? You *must* carry on. You are a great composer. Your music brings happiness to people. Don't die. Don't allow them to kill you!" Our conversation ended without any solution to our problem. We could only face the fact that to the Khmer Rouge, a human life was equal to a watermelon.

A couple of days later the cooperative leader requested a concert. As night came, we lit some torches and put them around our hut. When one started to burn out, we took a small stick and lit another. We played music and Svay cried. The cooperative leader came and sat on the small rise and listened to the music. Because it was dark and she was wearing black clothes, I couldn't see her face at all. I could only hear her voice calling out for another song. After a while we rested and I went to urinate in the forest. The leader stopped me and said, "Daran, who is the mandolin player?"

"That is Svay Sam Oeur."

"He looks old. Tomorrow I'll send him to work in the kitchen."

"But tomorrow the soldiers want to kill him for eating a watermelon."

"I will see that that does not happen."

Svay was happy to hear that. The next morning he was feeling better. The children had spent the night and were sitting around a fire. Svay taught them a funny song, then left for his new assignment. I was sad to see him go but our paths were to cross once again.

During our time in Kraing Chapay, the other musicians and I were sometimes allowed to travel around the province to play for gatherings organized by the Khmer Rouge leaders. I found some happiness in this because at last I was free to play my music. Though the songs were not of my choosing, it was nonetheless music that had emerged from someone's imagination and spirit. It seemed that music, whatever its origin, was a life-giving force. At these gatherings people would express great curiosity about my accordion. Everyone loved its sound and that love was transferred to me. Crowds of people, children especially, followed me wherever I went to touch my accordion or beg for a song. Everywhere I went people gave me food or medicine or some other small gift that represented a sacrifice.

One time an old man asked me, "Are you Daran?"

"Yes," I answered.

The man said, "I was standing at the back of the crowd and I saw you tear open the chest."

"What do you mean?" I asked.

"Tear open the chest," he repeated impatiently.

"What are you referring to?" I asked him.

"I am referring to music!" He motioned with his arms.

"Oh, I see, grandfather. Yes, I can play the accordion."

"Will you play again?"

"Yes," I told him. "Sometime soon."

He gave a big toothless smile and went on his way, and I was left with an image of myself tearing open my chest. But playing music was like that: exposing my heart, laying myself open for all to see.

I recall thinking as I played before a sea of people that I could not see individuals anymore. Everyone looked alike in their formless black clothes and their skeletons. Even the young looked old. I thought of how long it had been since I'd seen any display of affection between men and women or even between children and their parents. No one made love anymore. The desire was gone. Nor was there any comfort in making love—just hard bones hitting against bones. Consequently no women glowing with pregnancy and no joyful cry of newborn babies. All the death might have been easier to accept if children were being born. There is a sadness unlike any other when you see life's continuum coming to an end. It means nothing less than the end of the world.

Around me I saw people who had become so exhausted, so broken by the terror in Cambodia, that they resigned themselves to death. Indeed, they welcomed it as a way to end their suffering. For them sleep was easy. But I could not give myself up to that fate. Instead I napped in the evening so I could stay alert during the night. Midnight or the early morning hours were the favorite times for the soldiers to come and quietly take someone to the forest to kill. Even now, many years later, I awake at midnight to see if I am still alive.

The killing was always in secret. But it was not difficult to know who the executioners were. They were the ones with the red eyes and trembling hands. With them I was most careful.

Let me talk about nightfall. Night was the time of fear. Night was the time when, in the dark, all of us saw with clarity our fears, our aloneness, our loss, and our powerlessness against our own murderous brothers. Night was the time when the invisible had more power than the physical.

The fear of night did not begin when it got dark. It began at the first signs of fading light. I remember cursing the setting sun as it faded away: "Don't go! Don't go!"

The sleep of a Cambodian was memory-filled sleep. I slept near the levee of the rice field. And as I slept I could hear the cry of a cow over and over again and the wind in the trees like my mother's singing. I slept under the shadow of a tree. The tree was filled with sweet fruit. The wind carried the scent to me: the scent of my mother. I was reminded of everything and it was as though the levee broke and I slept and cried, slept and cried.

The end of my time at Kraing Chapay came with a soldier's announcement that I had a new assignment. I put my accordion on my back and my spoon in my waistband. I said to the other men, "I am leaving now with many memories of you. If you see my parents someday, tell them what happened to me." We all cried, and as I walked away they called out to me, "Go with safety, brother." I felt the heaviness of the moment and even before I reached the road, I composed a song in my head, a song I call "Kraing Chapay."

Fate gave me one beautiful moment of insight. On the night after I had left Kraing Chapay, the men in my new cooperative began to talk about the killing and the talk upset us and made us fearful. For no reason at all, I said to them, "You need not worry. Do you see that bird in the tree above us? Do you hear its voice? I can understand its language. I learned it when I lived in the forest. I will translate for you. It is saying, 'I will protect you. Believe me. Believe in me.'" This gave us relief and we lay down to sleep.

In that cooperative, people slept together in hammocks made of rice sacks. We arranged them around a tree like spokes coming out of a wheel. Before lying down to sleep we always started a fire to warm us and keep the mosquitoes away. Some time later that night I awoke and found my hammock and blanket on fire. I jumped up at once and found I was not badly burned, but I had only half a hammock and half a blanket left. I lay back down exhausted but unable to sleep. I said to the heavens, "Why am I always having bad luck? Do you want to punish me? To kill me by fire?"

There was no answer. But after some thought I began to see that bad luck, fire, and cold had forced me to wake many times during the night—and when I woke to add wood to the fire, its warmth and light comforted me. I realized too that for a long time no one in my unit had been killed—and that was because I was awake and the Khmer Rouge never wanted anyone to see them take someone to kill. And sitting quietly under the night sky, I remembered my time in the forest sitting in the treetop watching over the other men. I saw that again I had been the eyes of the sleeping and the keeper of the flame. I forgave the gods for my misfortune.

Once when I did sleep I had a dream. In the dream, Prince Sihanouk came to me and said, "I will die soon and you must take over as king of Cambodia."

"How can I do that?" I asked. "I am poor. I have no power."

He replied, "When the time comes, you will know."

The days passed in the dream and then Prince Sihanouk came to see me. As he walked through the door he stabbed his forehead on a nail sticking out of the doorway. He fell to the ground, blood pouring out of his head, and lay dying. I ran to him and held him in my arms. I asked him, "Why didn't you bend down when you saw the nail?!"

The prince said, "I am too old. My eyes cannot see and I cannot bend."

During that period of my life I had many dreams. The recurring theme was returning to my home in Pursat. In one such dream I arrived home to see my parents and my brothers and my sister once again—all healthy and laughing and glowing with life. The trees of the farm were full of colorful fruit and the rice crop was heavy. I saw my mother and said to her, "I told everyone you were dead, but you are not." My mother hugged me and said, "Of course I am not dead. Now, go get your brothers so we can have a concert for the gods." I went to get my brothers. They opened the closet to take out their instruments and there, in the closet, was a generator producing a bright light. We had not known it was there and we delighted in its presence. We played music then and filled the sky with our joy. Such life! Everywhere such life!

Always I woke from these dreams knowing I had been dreaming but I could not stop the feeling that for a short time I had been enveloped by my family. The comfort of dreams sustained me.

In Cambodia it is very important to honor one's ancestors and the spirits. The Khmer Rouge, however, attempted to replace religion with materialism. They destroyed the temples and told the monks, "Take off your orange robes and go to work. You can't just sit around anymore letting the people serve you." They did not allow funeral rites and the burning of incense. They forced the Cham people, who are Muslim, to eat pork and buried them upside down. The April 17 people were fearful about carrying out rituals, but we managed to do so secretly. We were not allowed to burn incense, but whenever we sat around a fire we watched the rising smoke and said our silent prayers.

One's spirituality is a difficult thing to contain—even for the most devoted cadres. I witnessed the Khmer Rouge still acting out the rituals taught to them as children. For instance, there is a ritual in Cambodian society that every child knows called *"reasay,"* which translates to something like "honor." This ritual began long ago when a boy and girl were resting under a tree and seeking advice from God. The advice came from the voice of the birds who said, "A person washes his face upon awakening to start the day clean. At midday he washes his chest to remove the dirt of his character. And at night he washes off the spoiled scent of the feet." Cambodian people perform this ritual without thinking.

Even the Khmer Rouge, who disregarded religious teaching, did it without thought. This made me recognize them as Cambodians.

The link between blood and spirituality lies deep in the human mind. But unlike spiritual matters, blood is a physical manifestation. When I think of my time under the Khmer Rouge, I think of blood. Blood was an obsession with them. The national anthem of Democratic Kampuchea, our country's name under the Khmer Rouge regime, was this:

> Red red blood splatters the cities and plains of the
> Cambodian fatherland,
> The sublime blood of workers and peasants,
> The blood of revolutionary fighters of both sexes.
> Blood spills out into great indignation and a resolute
> urge to fight.
> On April 17, that day under the revolutionary flag,
> Blood liberated us from slavery.

When the Khmer Rouge ruled, blood did run in Cambodia, not in a trickle, not in a stream, but in a violent torrent. Why blood was always on the lips and hands of the Khmer Rouge I do not know. I doubt if the Khmer Rouge soldiers themselves even knew. It came from something deep in the human mind, maybe something we are born with, a thirst for blood or the knowledge that blood makes us brothers. It is not surprising, then, that the liver, an organ filled with blood, took on great importance to the Khmer Rouge. They had a practice of cutting out and eating the liver of the people they killed because they believed it could make them strong and prevent them from getting malaria or other diseases.

One day one of the soldiers said to me, "Drink this coconut water. It has liver in it to make you strong. Drink it so you can work harder."

The thought of this disgusted me but I did not feel free

to refuse it. I said to him, "I am not well today. I feel dizzy. If I drink this I might vomit and I would regret wasting it." He said something to me but I looked past him as though I was distracted. When he asked me what I was thinking about, I said, "Oh, I am just reminded of a story."

"What story?" he asked. I was lying, of course. I had no story. But from nowhere a story came into my head. It was a story from India, an *"abul kasem"* we called it, which is a never-ending story. I began to talk: There once was a man who traveled to faraway places and met many people along the way, and each of them had their own story to tell . . . and at the end of his journey he met an old woman who said, "You are mistaken, for you see. . . ." On and on I went, one story inside another, inside another, the voice of one character after another coming out of my mouth. I have no idea where the words came from.

The soldier was a young, uneducated man, probably only twenty, and from a remote area of northeastern Cambodia. He became fascinated with my story and sat down to listen. I talked and talked, transforming myself from one character into another. I changed my stance, my voice, my vocabulary. The soldier listened until it was dark. He laughed at my dramatic conclusion and got up to go. When he stood up, he accidentally knocked over the coconut with the liver in it. I watched it pour out and soak into the ground.

As the months went on, my will to go on living began to wane. Every day death took another person by starvation, disease, or murder. Then the last of the men I had been with in the forest died. I thought it was my turn.

I sat on the ground thinking of the sadness of my life and for no reason began to dig a hole. As I sat looking at this hole, the image of a drum entered my head. I gathered some sticks and string and made a drum and played it. It had a deep, rich sound which vibrated outward. Soon, children appeared by my side to listen and see how I had made the drum. People swam across the river to find out where the sound was coming from. They said, "That's not a drum. A drum must be made of wood and sit above the ground." I played some more and before long, everyone was dancing and letting out little shouts of joy. They pounded their feet on the ground causing a great cloud of dust to rise up. I looked at the cloud and saw it mix with the rising spirit of my people. I sat with this image knowing it was good. I played a funny little song then and the children began to laugh, which in our culture is a sign there will be peace.

A few days later, I heard the sounds of drums. People in other villages had made the same drum. Drumming came from all directions. It was a strong, steady sound like heartbeats. I sat in the middle as if I were the stone that had been thrown in the water causing these ripples of sound. I listened and I was happy.

Happiness was not mine for long, however. The children were laughing but the Khmer Rouge could not hear because they did not stop their killing and there still was no peace in Cambodia. A dreadful thing happened to me during this time—something that still causes me terrible nightmares. One day the soldiers gathered up the people of the cooperative and took us to the forest. They ordered us to take sticks and hit the trees and beat the ground to scare any animals out of their hiding places. On the perimeter of the area the soldiers stood ready with guns to kill any animals that emerged.

My father used to do this when I was young and always instructed me to stand and move just so, so that I would not be shot. I whispered to the others, "Be careful you are not shot. Make sure there's a tree nearby so that when an animal runs out you can run to the tree for protection. These soldiers don't care if they shoot you. It makes no difference to them." They listened and nodded and we proceeded to walk in the forest and hit the trees and shout. Each time an animal ran out, we all hid behind the trees. But once, as I ran to a tree, I fell into a huge hole.

It was not exactly a hole. It was an open grave of people murdered by the Khmer Rouge. Suddenly the terror of the night was seen in the light of day. The hole was soft and muddy from the blood and decomposing bodies. The bodies were in varying degrees of decomposition. Some of the faces, though, were still intact with frozen expressions of terror. I stood half sunk in a sea of rotting body parts, sickened by the image and the smell. I was not merely seeing it, I was immersed in it. I was standing in death so deep I could not move.

Someone came to pull me out. And though I was not hurt, my mind was deeply affected. For weeks afterward I felt the overwhelming despair of life in Cambodia. After that I could hardly go on. I kept pinching myself to see if I was still alive. My mind was consumed with thoughts of those bodies in the pit. I wondered where their souls had gone without proper burial from their children. Even now I wonder if they have made it into the next life or if they are still in that pit in Cambodia.

It was laughter, somehow, that pulled me out of my despair. This is how it happened. I went with six other men to get honey from a tree on the opposite side of the lake. The particular bees we planned to take the honey from were big and mean, so before we climbed the tree we carried out a ritual to protect us from danger. The two oldest men chanted to the sky: "We believe in nature. Bees, we take this from you because we need it for our life. Do not harm us. Good spirits, protect us." We then made a torch by stuffing dried leaves inside a length of bamboo. I climbed the tree first and two men followed me. With their buckets ready they waited.

We had bad luck that day. The fire burned too fast and there was not enough smoke. The bees began to attack us. We swung our arms about wildly. Then I fell on the man below me, we both fell on the man below him, and then all three of us hit the ground. We got up and ran to the nearby village with great swarms of bees in pursuit.

When the villagers saw us, they yelled, "Don't come this way!" I ran into a house and climbed under a mosquito net where several other people were gathered. It was so crowded we were pressed against the sides and the bees kept stinging us. So I escaped from there and ran into a chicken coop. But I could not get away from those bees! Finally, the three of us ran into the granary and buried ourselves in some rice. At last we were safe.

When we emerged, in great pain, we found the villagers waiting for us. They had sticks and an angry stance. One of them came raging toward me and raised his stick. "I want to kill you!" he yelled. I looked at his face. It was ridiculous! His left eye was swollen shut, his right cheek was puffed out, and he had a huge, swollen red nose. I burst into laughter. "Why are you laughing?" he demanded.

"You look so funny!"

"Well, you look funny yourself with your puffed-out body."

Indeed my lips were so swollen they reached my nose and chin. A small laugh escaped from the man's body. Seeing him laugh made me laugh again, and before long everyone was laughing. We fell to the ground and tears streamed out of our eyes. With the laughter we forgot our troubles. We felt a lightness of heart none of us had experienced in a long time.

Our assignments were always being changed. The section leader would just come and say, "Today you will go work somewhere else."

My next assignment was to work in the rice fields and tend the cows. That was in 1977, the worst year of all under the Khmer Rouge. They executed great numbers of people that year, one by one in the rural areas and by the hundreds at Tuol Sleng, the torture center in Phnom Penh, where people were sent to make confessions. *"Tuol Sleng"* means "Hill of the Poison Fruit." It had been a high school before the Khmer Rouge turned it into a hell.

I want to tell you a story about that time. It is a story about my mother and a spoon. We were constantly being reminded by our leaders not to think of ourselves but only about society. Most people were only allowed to own two things: a bowl and a spoon. I carried my spoon in the waistband of my pants so I would be prepared to eat at the designated time. Food had been rationed in 1975 and 1976, yet everyone was allowed to prepare their own food. Beginning in late 1976, however, food became so scarce we were told we would have to eat at a central location—and only what we were given. The cooperatives were organized by "kitchens." There were five hundred to a thousand people to each kitchen.

One day during the rainy season I was plowing the rice field in water up to my knees. I noticed some fish and crabs in the water. I picked them up quickly so no one would notice and I put them in my pants. When no one was looking, I took them to the forest, wrapped them in leaves, and buried them in the ground. I returned to the field and continued plowing until I heard the kitchen leaders banging the bottom of a bowl, the signal to eat.

That day, as on most days, we were being given hot rice soup for our meal. When I reached in my pants for my spoon it was not there! I did not know what to do. Because there was a shortage of everything, I knew it would be impossible to get another spoon. I returned to the field thinking I must have dropped my spoon when I was picking up the fish and crabs. I returned to the plow and hit the buffalo to get him moving again. I went over and over in the field looking through the mud and water for my spoon but I couldn't see it. A soldier called out, "Look at our hardworking comrade! He wants to keep working for Angkar!"

I was watching the parting of the water while going over in my mind what to do. Maybe I could make a spoon from a piece of wood, but that could take a long time—and besides I had no knife. Or maybe I could fold a leaf just so, as my mother had taught me to do. Yes, I thought I could do that. As I watched the parting of the water, a strange feeling came over me. I began to talk to my mother: "Yes, Mother. I remember now when I was a small brown boy running out to the yard to get a leaf. You said to me, 'Daran, take this kind of leaf. It is the strongest. Fold it here, then here.' And taking it to where you were cooking sugar water, I scraped out the sweet, crusted sides of the empty bowl. Yes, Mother, I hear you. That is what I will do."

Just then I saw my spoon. When I returned to the kitchen, there was no more soup. But one of the others said, "Here, Daran. We have each saved a spoonful for you." Each put a spoonful of soup in my bowl. When I had finished eating I whispered to them, "Now after our work is finished, come with me." At the end of the day, the others came to me and I led them to the forest. I dug up the ground, revealed the fish and crabs, and said, "Now let's eat again." They all smiled and one said, "Only you could find fish on the land!" This made us laugh and we ate together and were reminded of what it was like not to be hungry.

The rice fields of Cambodia are rich with the spirits of my people. I can tell you of one of those spirits, a man named Mr. Sorn. Mr. Sorn was not an extraordinary man. He was not even a talented man. He was just a good man who breathed and worked and took care of his family. One day Mr. Sorn was plowing the rice field. As he plowed I was walking behind him planting rice seedlings. While we worked, Khmer Rouge soldiers sat on the bank and hit us with a whip if we were too slow or made mistakes. I looked up and saw that Mr. Sorn, who had become desperately thin, had lost hold of his plow. The cow just kept walking, dragging him through the mud. I went to him; his mouth and nose were already filled with mud. I picked him up and carried him to the edge of the rice field. A soldier said, "Daran, go back to work!" I ignored him and tried to take the mud out of Mr. Sorn's mouth. The soldier came closer and raised his whip. "Go back to work now."

So I left Mr. Sorn there in the rice field to die. Many people died in the rice fields. It was almost as if they wanted to die where they had grown the food that made them live. It was like completing a cycle.

Days passed. The section leader came and told me I would be one of those sent to cut bamboo. This involved a difficult journey of three days up a mountain. Once we reached the place, we cut bamboo, made a raft, and floated a load of bamboo down the Pursat River where another group of people took it over. Then we returned to the forest to cut more bamboo.

I remember the orange trees lining the banks of the river. The oranges looked delicious, but to take any of the fruit without permission was to invite a death sentence. Besides, our raft was too swift and the trees passed by too quickly. So we floated down the river looking at oranges, round and sweet and seductive, just beyond our reach. Oranges we could not have.

One time while we were cutting bamboo, the weather grew stormy. There were great flashes of lightning and the earth rumbled violently. Despite the bad weather, I continued cutting the bamboo. While I was at the top, maybe twenty meters high, a great wind came up and the bamboo began to sway back and forth. For fifteen or twenty minutes I managed to hold on but then I grew tired and fell. But I didn't fall to the ground. As I fell, my belt caught on the sharpened end of the bamboo I had just cut. The bamboo cut my belly but hooked my belt so that I was left hanging from the tree with blood running down my legs. I could not turn around to see what was holding me. Neither could I reach any branches to pull myself free. I hung helplessly suspended, hanging by a thread, bobbing like a buoy in the sea.

After a while, I heard the others and called to them. They could not believe my good fortune. "When we fall from a tree, we hit the ground. But you just hover above! Does that bamboo love you?" They laughed, and then one of them stood on the shoulder of another and cut me down and I fell into the arms of the third. The four of us sat together while the thunder shook the ground and the rain poured over our bodies. When it stopped, we loaded our raft with bamboo and floated it down the river to a place where I was to hear news about my family.

As I unloaded the bamboo into a cart, I noticed the driver staring at me. Then he whispered close to my face, "Do you know Sonn?"

"Sonn? Who is that?"

"His face looks like yours. He told me he has a brother but he doesn't know where he is."

"His name is Sonn?" I asked.

"Yes."

"No, I don't know anyone named Sonn."

"Why do you look just like him then? You must know him."

"How do you know this man Sonn?" I asked.

"I used to play soccer with him. He was a professional soccer player. Are you sure you don't know him? He is the same size as you, maybe a year or two older. His mother's name is Hoeun." My heart began to beat faster as I realized he was describing my brother Reatrey. My grandmother had called him Sonn.

I said, "I only know someone like that named Reatrey."

"Yes! Reatrey! That was his name before. Is he your brother?"

"Yes! I am his brother, Daran. You know Reatrey? You know where he is?"

"Yes, I do. He and your mother, your sister, and your brothers live in Kandeang district."

"My father, where is he?" I asked impatiently.

"Your father was killed in 1975. I'm sorry."

After a moment I said, "And Chamroeun?"

"Chamroeun and Bunly and Dararith, nobody can find them."

"Dararith lives near me!"

It was easy to guess that my father had been killed. But it was hard to hear the words come out in someone's voice. I stood on the road feeling alone. Then I went into the forest, so no one could see me, and cried for my father. I sat among the chhleach and mango trees near a pond and recalled every memory I had of my father. In particular, I remembered New Year's celebrations he organized for the poor. Cambodians celebrate the New Year in April: a time of great feasts, musicians filling the air with song, beautiful dancers, games for the children. In one game, my father used a slingshot to throw coins to the crowd. Everyone jumped up to catch them, shouting with joy or disappointment. I, the happy little boy, stood nearby to replenish his supply. My father would always give a speech to encourage people and make them feel bright and brave. At sunset came the most important event of the day. My father would write the names of gifts on small pieces of paper, fold them, and tie them to a tree with thread. Each person attending the celebration chose one. The gifts were such things as silk cloth or jewelry or bags of rice. But on one piece of paper was my father's name. When that paper was chosen, the drummer drummed loudly and dramatically and the people grew quiet. The drums sounded like the gods coming down to earth to sit among the people. The orchestra played, too, so that the sound filled the space between people, making us one.

Whoever picked the paper with my father's name received my father's soul. It then became necessary for my father to buy it back with ten thousand riel, because he was not ready to let his soul fly away. There was always a formal and deeply felt greeting between my father and the person who chose his name, as they acknowledged that we sometimes hold the life of another in our hands. They would hug for a long time, and someone would throw jasmine flowers on them. The exchange was made, the crowd cheered, and my father cried out with happiness, "I'm still alive! I'm still alive!"

Among the trees I cried for a long while. Then I told myself the Buddhist proverb: "Free thyself from the past, free thyself from the future, free thyself from the present. Crossing to the farther shore of existence, with mind released everywhere, no more shalt thou come to birth and decay."

When the cart driver, Dara, returned to my family he told them he had met me. Dara told me they were inexpressibly happy, especially my mother.

My brother Reatrey was a skillful person and useful to the Khmer Rouge. Because of his usefulness, he had some power not granted to the rest of the April 17 people. Or maybe it was a trick of the Khmer Rouge to have Reatrey identify his family. Anyway, he was given permission to take me and Dararith from our cooperative so we could be with our mother. By coincidence, the day I was to meet Reatrey again happened to be the day I was sent to cut mysuck trees. Before I cut any trees, however, I cried. Why should I cry about cutting a tree? Because when I saw those trees, I saw my family.

I could remember the day when my father called a family meeting to discuss an idea Reatrey had. His idea was to plant mysuck trees on our land alongside the road. My father asked: "Why should we plant this tree?" We took turns answering.

"We can use its wood to make the butt of a gun."

"But let's not use it for weapons. Its wood is excellent for making furniture."

"And we can use it to make a beautiful house for everyone to see."

"It will give shade to passersby on the road."

"It makes excellent violins and guitars."

"Its wood is strong but light and easy to carry."

"It is easy to grow. Even if we don't water it, it will stay alive."

My father again: "Yes, let's plant one tree for each member of our family."

So we had a celebration to reward Reatrey for his good idea and planted eleven trees to represent the eleven members of our family.

The Khmer Rouge did not want to cut those trees for the lumber. They only wanted to burn them. Why did they want to destroy the mysuck tree? It was not their enemy. As I cut the trees I was unaware that Reatrey was passing by looking for me. At the end of the day, I returned to the village. One of the soldiers asked me to play the piano and it was while I was playing that Reatrey found me.

For a long time we embraced each other. Then Reatrey showed us the permit allowing us to go see our family. I held the permit and danced with excitement. Reatrey had come on a bicycle and I asked a soldier for two more bicycles. I told him we had been given permission to go to Kandeang district. "Let me see it!" he demanded. My brother handed the permit to him. The soldier held it upside down and pretended to read it. "Okay," he said, and told me where to get the bicycles.

Once we had prepared to go, Dararith and I said good-bye to the people we knew and the three of us set off in the direction of our home. Dararith and I were elated at the idea of seeing our mother and brothers and sister. We had gone not thirty meters, however, when suddenly my bicycle tire exploded and I fell to the ground. I lay there, saying to the sky, "Again, God, you punish me!" My brothers stopped and looked at me. Dararith began to cry because he wanted to see our mother. I told Reatrey, "Take Dararith and go. I will try to repair my bicycle and you can come for me later." I knew that bicycle parts were hard to get and it might be many weeks before I could go, but I pretended it would not be long. I hugged them both good-bye and watched as they pedaled down the road and turned.

Many weeks passed and I heard nothing from Reatrey or his friend Dara, the cart driver. Finally, one day as I was washing my face, I heard the cart coming. I ran to Dara and asked, "Why hasn't Reatrey come back for me?" At first, he said nothing. He simply got down from the cart. "Daran, Reatrey has had some trouble. He's been sent away to work at the blacksmith cooperative in Som San village." The words felt foreboding. Som San means "Mournful Place."

"How is the rest of my family? Was my mother happy to see Dararith?

Dara did not say anything. I put my face close to his. "Tell me," I said.

"I don't want to say anything," he said.

I said calmly, "Let me go cut some sugarcane for you to take back to them. My little sister Raksmey loves sugarcane."

Dara stopped me and said, "Daran, your family has been killed."

At first I couldn't say anything. Then I asked him, "Why were they killed? What happened?"

Dara told me they found out that my mother had been the wife of the chief of police and they accused her of being Vietnamese. They hadn't killed her at first because they saw she was knowledgeable about agriculture. But then they found out. So they raped her and shot her afterwards.

I picked up my saw and began to cut a log. Then Dara told me how each of my family members had died. I felt faint from the images his words produced. I dropped the saw and it cut my finger. I watched little drops of my blood fall to the ground. It was at that moment that I became a ghost.

Dara told me he would not be returning to see me anymore. I walked into the forest and began beating my head against a tree. I wanted to die. I thought of how I might kill myself. I thought I might take a knife and cut the tender undersides of my arms and let my life drain from my body and soak into the earth. Then a child appeared and asked, "Uncle, can you play your accordion tonight? We want to dance."

"No, little one," I said. "I do not have the strength." She left and returned to me with a tiny handful of bamboo shoots and put them up to my mouth. I ate them and then she asked, "Now can you play?"

She was tiny and sweet like my sister Raksmey. I looked at her for a short time, then said, "Yes, I will play for you, little child. For you I will play." I picked up my accordion and I played. The music kept death from me for one more day.

The rainy season began with hatred for my people. Day after day went by without any break from the heavy downpour. Crops began to rot. Our damp clothes clung to our bodies so that our bones showed through. The dark clouds lay low and heavy in the sky and the rain extinguished our night fires. Our bodies shook with cold in our sleep.

The rain made the mosquitoes breed, too, and this led to an outbreak of a deadly form of malaria. Each day another person was taken by the disease. The mosquitoes were especially bad in the forested areas. Each time my group went back into the bush to cut bamboo, another man fell victim to the malaria. At last there were only two of us making the trip to cut bamboo.

Despite the bad weather, another man and I succeeded in reaching the bamboo grove and we spent a whole day cutting. At nightfall, he complained of a headache and during the night his body began to shake violently next to mine. I knew then that he too had gotten malaria. I sat with him for a while trying to comfort him. Sweat poured from his body. He died the next evening. I was alone.

The next morning I loaded the bamboo on the raft and climbed onto it. The river was very swift, though, and the raft could barely keep afloat. I could see I wouldn't be able to steer it myself, so I jumped off and watched as the current took the raft and crashed it against the rocks. I swam to shore. I thought I would just walk back, but the heavy rain and my emotions disoriented me and I got lost. After a day or two, my stomach was burning from hunger. I searched everywhere but could find nothing to eat. So I sat down, thought about what I should do, and fell asleep.

When I woke, I began to remember a story told to me when I was a child. There once was a young boy who lived in a remote village. When the boy was six years old his father died and when he was seven years old death claimed his mother—both victims of a disease that had spread throughout the village. Out of fear the surviving villagers had moved away, leaving the boy alone.

This boy had only one possession: a knife, a *"kombet"* it was called. It had a razor-sharp blade and a long handle so that it could be carried on his back. He carried it everywhere. He taught himself to make a fish trap by stripping bark from trees and molding it into string that he attached to sticks. Catching fish was how he lived. But when he was fifteen years old, it seemed all the fish from his small lake had been caught, so he left his village to journey to another place.

The boy walked for many days with little to eat. Finally he came to a place next to the sea. He was happy because he had heard that the sea was full of fish. The boy went into the jungle nearby and gathered the materials to make a huge trap. He then placed the trap in the water. Almost immediately he caught a fish, which he roasted over a fire. The smell of the smoke awakened the sea king, however, who rose out of the water and demanded to know how such a small boy could catch such a big fish.

"I caught it in this trap I made with this string and these sticks I took from the land," said the boy.

"But how could that be strong enough to hold a fish?"

"It is strong, I assure you. Get in the trap and see for yourself."

The sea king could not resist a challenge and got in the trap saying, "If I am able to get out, I will eat you." But he couldn't; the trap was too strong. The sea king became angry with the boy. The boy delighted in the game and pretended he was going to roast the sea king and eat him and use his teeth to make a necklace. The sea king begged the boy to let him go. He promised that if he let him go, he would give him a magic white scarf. Simply by waving this scarf he would be granted any wish he wanted. The boy agreed, took the scarf, and released the king. When the king returned to the sea, he left behind him a trail of leaves which had fallen on him while he was on the earth. When the sea king got home he was exhausted and told everyone in his kingdom that if they woke him up he would kill them. He then went to sleep for one hundred years.

Meanwhile, the boy became very curious about the sea king's world. He gathered his courage and walked into the sea, following the trail of leaves the sea king had left. Under the sea, he came to a locked door. He waved the magic scarf and an army of men appeared and broke down the door. He came to another door and again he waved the scarf and the army of men appeared and broke down the door. He did this again and again until he came to the one hundred and first door. When that door was broken down, the boy saw the sea king sleeping. The boy waved the scarf. Great drummers appeared and beat their drums loudly and woke the king up. For a moment, the king was angry. Then he recognized the boy's bravery at daring to wake him up and the king submitted to him. The boy became the king, and the king was his servant. But a time came when the boy no longer wanted to be king. He returned to his village and never wanted for anything again.

I told myself: "Daran, you are that boy. You must go deep

in the ocean and face the sea king. But who is your sea king? And where is your white scarf and your drummers?" Then I heard the voices of men and the sound of a drum. I called to them and a group of men came to me. One of them was carrying a drum he had made to entertain them while they hunted for mushrooms. They helped me back to the village where I ate some rice and realized it was not yet my time to die.

How could I allow myself to die when I still had the strength to save myself and help others? An opportunity to do so came when I was given an assignment to collect supplies and distribute them to the people in the cooperatives. This assignment involved going into the town of Pursatville, which had been declared off limits once the Khmer Rouge were in power. Two Khmer Rouge soldiers and I took a truck into town. They rode in front and I in back. As we drove through the countryside, after a while I realized we were getting closer to my family's house. My heart beat faster, and I thought, "Almost there! I am almost there!" I wanted to cry. As we approached, I looked in the distance and saw that my house had been dismantled and the trees all cut down. It was a ghostly place with only the souls of my family, not their physical bodies. As we passed, I was reminded again of the magnitude of my loss.

The truck kept moving down the road and then all I could see were my father's initials "K. B." on the gateposts, carved deeply into the rock with the thousand shapes. The truck kept moving and the image got smaller and smaller, then disappeared.

When we reached town, no one was there except Khmer Rouge soldiers. I was given a Khmer Rouge uniform to wear, and we went to a warehouse to collect fifty-kilogram bags of cement. The warehouse was full of things: food, gold, colorful clothing, and musical instruments. I saw rats running about and eating the food. A group of soldiers sat at a table. They told me I could eat anything I wanted. I saw a bowl of sugar. Sugar has no scent yet I could smell it. The soldiers laughed and ate. One of them spilled some sugar on the floor. I couldn't stop looking at that sugar, and the rats eating the food, and thinking of the starving people in the cooperatives.

The soldiers motioned to me to join them. I hesitated. How could I eat when others were starving? Then something strange happened. I heard my grandmother call my name. I saw my grandmother talking to my father, urging him to join the Khmer Rouge. "My son, you must join them or they will kill you. I cannot allow you to die. Please, adjust your mind a little. Those soldiers don't want to lose the war."

Then I saw myself as a young boy. My grandmother was talking to my father. She was serving him little lemon cakes topped with sugar. While the two of them talked, I ate one cake after another. Sugar went into my veins, so much sugar that my heart started thumping fast. I felt my heart enlarge, I became aware of its strength.

In my mind I thanked my grandmother and returned to the present. I joined the Khmer Rouge by putting handfuls of sugar in my mouth. Soon I felt my heart, the strength of life, beating in my chest. Yes, I joined the Khmer Rouge. But not in their killing. I joined them in their living.

The things that filled the warehouse had arrived by train. And things that left Cambodia went out on the train. At night I went with the soldiers to the train station. There rice produced in the rural areas was being put on a train for China.

One day Angkar came to check on the exports; it was a Chinese man. I was told, "Be careful, work hard, and don't look at Angkar's face."

I had to pick up a fifty-kilogram bag of rice and carry it on my shoulder across a board that was propped against the train. I did this many times while the soldiers counted and recorded the bags. One time when I stepped on the board, it cracked and I fell. I hurt my back and could not move. The Chinese man squatted down next to me. He spoke through a translator. "Who is your group leader?"

I told him his name.

"Didn't he tell you to be careful?"

"I was careful, but the wood broke," I replied.

He said, "You should have known it would break. Don't you know the sound of breaking wood?"

I did not answer. I thought I would be killed. I simply got up and continued to load rice on the train.

That is why my people were so hungry. The Chinese thought the rice belonged to them. After that I began a dangerous practice: I began to share food. The soldiers and I collected food from the warehouses and I'd ride in the back of a truck past all the cooperatives and villages. When I saw someone I knew, I'd break open a bag of rice and let it trail off onto the road. Not just when I saw someone I knew, but when I saw the face of suffering. That face—it was just the look of that face that caused me to break open the bag of rice. The people when they saw this ran to the road and gathered the rice in their hands.

At that time my compassion grew. I don't know why. It was against my survival instinct to have compassion. Maybe it was something my father taught me. Maybe it was in my mind when I was born. In any case, there was a jail across the road from where I slept. The Khmer Rouge took people there to interrogate them. Once one of the prisoners escaped and eight or ten soldiers caught him on the road and surrounded him. One soldier hit him and threw him into another soldier. They all took turns hitting the man until he was nearly dead. Expecting him to die, the soldiers buried him in a shallow grave and left.

Since it was nightfall, I could go to the man without being seen. I pushed the dirt back and I saw his face. His head was bloody. He was still breathing but with difficulty. He said slowly, "Don't kill me."

"No, no, no! I want to save you. I want to save you. Maybe we'll end up in the grave together, but I want to help you."

The others in my group yelled for me to come back. I returned but I said, "I can't sleep. I want to help him."

"Okay. If you want to die, you can help him," they said.

I did not want to die but I could not stop feeling compassion. I took some water to the man and poured it on his face and gave him a drink. I said to him, "Wake up, wake up." He was struggling to breathe. I put my mouth over his and gave him my breath. I heard a Khmer Rouge soldier say, "Where is Daran?"

Someone said, "He went to urinate."

I tried once more to help the man breathe but he was growing weaker. Then I heard someone walking toward me. I left and went back to my hammock.

In the morning I returned to the man and found him dead. I heard a soldier approaching, the sound of his guns hitting his belt. To erase any evidence of my help, I pushed the dirt over the man without leaving any finger marks. I felt sorry, and tired, as if my own life was gone.

How brutal those soldiers were and how we all feared them. It would have been easy for me to think of them as faceless monsters devoid of human attributes. But the Khmer Rouge were humans. They were my fellow Cambodians who had grown up as I had on the rice and the fruit of our country. For this reason I tried to understand why they had lost the Cambodian characteristics of kindness and generosity. I knew their innocence made them easy prey for the Vietnamese communists. Those communists had made them accustomed to violence. Maybe it was an addiction they developed in the forest training when they had practiced killing animals.

But I suspected there was something more—some hidden pain, some vague anger, some emptiness. Or maybe it was just the path to survival they had chosen. Maybe they were as helpless as I, as caught up in the whirlpool of social change. I could not know because I could not talk to them about such things. I could only recognize aspects of their humanity and compare it to my own.

Let me tell you about one of these men. A soldier came to me one day and said, "There is a girl I love and I want to find out if she loves me. I order you to play your accordion for us." This was an unusual request from a soldier, but of course I agreed. I arranged for the soldier and the girl to meet. I played my accordion while sitting on the floor between them. As I played, they looked at each other. After a time I suggested they dance and they did. They danced beautifully. Then they began to sing a question and answer song back and forth. I could see they loved each other so I suggested they meet again.

The following week the soldier and the girl met again. They sat together inside the house while I hid underneath it. Through the slatted floor I could hear them talking sweetly. They sat close to each other but they were not kissing. I picked up a stick and poked the soldier to get his attention. He came outside and looked under the house.

"Why don't you kiss her?" I whispered to him.

"I am too shy. My heart is beating so fast," he said.

"If you don't kiss her she won't know you love her."

"I can't kiss her. Can't you see I am shaking with fear?"

I looked at his face, pointed my finger at him, and said in my firmest voice, "I order you to kiss her!"

He went back in and kissed the woman. I rolled over in quiet laughter and said to myself in disbelief, "Daran, you just gave orders to a Khmer Rouge soldier!" It was on that day I began to believe that, though it seemed impossible, maybe love was indeed stronger than the most brutal of men.

Daran with the accordion found on the stump of a tree during the time of the Khmer Rouge. (Photo: Janet Jensen)

Daran *(right)* with Mr. Chhoeun, a fellow musician.
(Photo: Janet Jensen)

Bree with Daran at the ancient temple of Angkor Wat.
(Photo: Janet Jensen)

V
Reconciliation

As the Khmer Rouge regime went on, life became more and more difficult. The killing and terror never stopped. There was never enough food, enough freedom, enough joy. The other April 17 people were so vulnerable to illness that there were many outbreaks of malaria, cholera, and other diseases. When I got malaria, I became so ill I could not work and was taken to the village to rest. While burning with a high fever and mad with headache, I saw my brother Chamroeun once again.

Lying on my stomach on the floor of the kitchen building, I looked up to see a figure walking toward me from fifty meters away. He looked like my brother Chamroeun. I thought I was dreaming or confused from my fever. I closed my eyes and opened them again. It was Chamroeun. He was very thin and small and he was crying and mucus ran out of his nose. He looked like a child, but I knew it was him because he was wearing the shorts my mother had made for him from the same material she had used for mine.

"Chamroeun!" I called. I pushed the blanket from my body and ran to him. "Where have you been?" I asked him.

"I've been in the forest," he said.

"Where are our parents?" I asked, forgetting they were dead.

"Oh, little brother, don't think about that now."

"What has happened to Cambodia?" I cried.

"Hush now, brother, and lie back down."

Chamroeun came close to me. At first we didn't know what to say to each other. Quietly he began to sing forbidden songs in my ears. "Do you remember these songs?"

I smiled. "Yes, yes. I remember."

Even though we were grown men, we slept together that night holding each other. In the morning I woke and looked at my brother's sleeping body. He was still wearing the necklace my father had given him. It was a small Buddha inside a box on a silver chain. My father had given it to Chamroeun to protect him from harm. I thought of my father and my mind filled with memories of our family.

I was overjoyed to see my brother again. And as I hugged him again, I heard the sounds of his empty stomach. "Brother, you are so thin. I must get something for you to eat," I said. I went to dig up a potato and pick an ear of corn I had grown myself. I returned to my brother and watched him eat the corn. I remember his face so clearly: the kernels of corn around his mouth mixed with the tears from his eyes; the sadness of his stories mixed with his gladness at finding me. My brother was so thin but so beautiful. So beautiful! You cannot imagine.

We began to talk. I learned that Chamroeun had been looking for me for a long time. After the last time I saw him, he had returned to his wife and children. He had then run away in April 1975 when he found out the Khmer Rouge were planning to kill him. He hid in the forest for many months and tried, as I did, to escape to Thailand, but he was unable to leave. He decided he would have to find a way to live in Cambodia under the Khmer Rouge.

Because of his experience being held hostage by the Khmer Rouge in 1971, he knew that paper and pen alone would ensure his survival in the new society. He left the forest, found paper and pen, and wrote out a permit in small print so neat it looked like it had been typewritten. It said something like: "Allow Kong Chamroeun to live and eat in your cooperative." So he traveled from cooperative to cooperative looking for our family. Chamroeun talked with sorrow about his wife Sophat, his son Tito, and his little daughters. The Khmer Rouge had already killed his daughters. He didn't know where his wife and son were.

While Chamroeun was talking, a woman suddenly appeared at the door with a soldier behind her. She pointed at me. "He is the one who took the corn!" I was scared but Chamroeun was calm and said to the soldier, "I have permission to eat here." He showed the soldier the paper. The soldier looked at it for a long time. "Okay. He can eat the corn."

Chamroeun told me he had met his old employee, Mr. Chhien, and that it was he who had told him where to find me. Mr. Chhien was then a section leader in a cooperative nearby. Chamroeun told me he would go to live with him and some of the Khmer Rouge soldiers. I did not like the idea of my brother living with the Khmer Rouge, but he believed no harm would come to him. Indeed, he thought it would be safer for him. I didn't want him to leave, but he left with a promise to return.

About five days later, he stood outside my hut and called to me, "Tooch! Tooch!" I had nearly forgotten my old nickname and smiled at the sound of it. I let my brother in and he gave me some palm sugar and tobacco. He told me he was living in the Leach district with the Khmer Rouge. "What do you do over there?" I asked him.

"I am a doctor," he said.

"How can you be a doctor?"

"I assisted the doctor who stayed with us when we were young, do you remember? That's all the training the Khmer Rouge require."

"Chamroeun! How can you live with the Khmer Rouge? That is like living with a sharp knife. You must be very careful."

Chamroeun spent the night with me. After that he visited me every few days. He walked across the forest at night and brought me sugar and other bits of food. He fed me like he was my mother and father. Once he took me to his hut. I saw his change of clothes hanging on the wall and the folding cot he slept on. "Look at this," he said to me. He removed the scarf from around his neck and unrolled it. The outline of our parents' feet was drawn on the scarf. "I wear this to feel them close to me," he said.

Once Chamroeun took me to the kitchen in his cooperative. "You can eat as much rice as you want," he whispered. But I could hardly eat because I knew it was food that was intended for someone as hungry as I. Chamroeun saw my hesitation, but he had a different idea. He looked into my eyes and spoke in a firm voice. "You eat this food. Just think of yourself, Daran. If you are going to die, you must have a reason to die, not just some little mistake. I will never die. I will always stay with you. I don't want you to die, so eat this food." Even in the Khmer Rouge time, when it wasn't easy to think, my brother was bright, especially about complicated things. It made no difference whether you thought of anything useful. It was of no consequence. You could use your mind to solve mathematical problems or questions of physics, but you could not solve the human problems or use your mind to end your suffering or that of those around you.

Yes, my brother was bright. But in the end even his brightness could not save him. I do not want to say what happened to him, the words are so bitter in my mouth.

Chamroeun told me he wanted to escape to Thailand. I argued with him and told him of my troubles in trying to cross the border, but in his desperation he would not listen to me. "It is just a matter of time before someone finds out we are brothers and we are educated," he said. "Do you think your accordion will always save you? We have no choice but to go."

We made a plan to meet on a particular night at the hut of Mr. Phat, one of the low-level leaders of the cooperative. I waited for my brother all night and grew more anxious with each hour that passed. At about 4:30 in the morning, I heard Chamroeun's voice. "I am sorry, Tooch. I couldn't come sooner. There were a lot of soldiers cleaning the forest." "Cleaning the forest" meant they were looking for people trying to escape. We decided to try again in a few days.

I waited and waited for Chamroeun's return, but he did not come for me. I needed to know what was wrong. After several days I borrowed a bicycle from Mr. Chhoeun and took a bag of oranges and went to Chamroeun's hut. When I arrived I did not see him. I saw a Khmer Rouge named Chon with whom Chamroeun had been living. "Where is Chamroeun?" I asked him.

"I don't know," he said.

I knew I should not ask questions but I needed to see Chamroeun. So I asked him again, "How can you live with Chamroeun and not know where he is?"

The man grew irritated and yelled at me, "He was sent away to cut bamboo."

I looked around and saw Chamroeun's scarf still hanging on the wall. I knew he would not go anywhere without it. Then . . . oh this image makes me cry . . . I looked under the cot where my brother slept and saw a small pool of blood. Then I saw blood splattered on the walls. I knew it was my brother's blood, and I felt sick, my heart frantic. I felt faint. I felt I might die. I looked at the man and knew he had killed my brother but I said nothing. I was scared then that he would kill me too and for a few moments I did not care. But something pushed me out of the hut.

I rode the bicycle along the dirt road and cried out for my brother's soul. I shouted his name over and over. Dust blew up into my face and mixed with my tears. When I returned to my hut, I put the oranges intended for my brother on a plate. I thought of my brother's talents, his beauty and compassion, his desire for life and justice. Finally I said a long prayer for him and wished him well in the next life. I left the oranges on that plate until they lost their glow and became rotten. Then I took them to the rice field where I buried them.

When I returned to my cooperative, my section leader said, "Where have you been?" I told him I had malaria and had stayed home to rest. He said he would ask Mr. Phat about that. He then summoned Mr. Phat and asked him why I had been absent. Mr. Phat was nervous. I prayed he would lie for me. "He was not feeling well," Mr. Phat said.

I was allowed to go. Down the road Mr. Phat looked at me with a long face and said, "If you were anyone else, today you would die."

I went back to work in the rice field. It was my assignment to take a string and measure out rows for the seedlings. That was an easy assignment for me. I had good eyesight and my mother had taught me how to measure land perfectly.

This work required that I look off into the distance. I held one end of the string while another man held the other end. As I looked at the horizon and the setting sun, Chamroeun's song about not knowing the future and not being able to reach the horizon returned to me. I sang that song quietly to myself and cried for my brother. I thought that my sorrow would surely kill me, but the comfort of death was still not to be mine.

Not long after that I was sent to work in a quarry high in the mountains of the Phnom Kravanh district. The Khmer Rouge sent us there to collect rocks to build dams along the Pursat

River. Work was very hard there. The rocks were all huge boulders and we didn't have the proper tools to break them apart. There was no shade and the rocks reflected the heat of the sun. The work took every bit of energy within our bodies. But it was a bit of good fortune that I was sent to the quarry because it was there I met the musician Svay Sam Oeur once again.

After Svay had left us at Kraing Chapay, he stayed in the kitchen and worked for only a week. Like me, he had had many other assignments before coming to the quarry. He was old and sick and could hardly work. It seemed he was sent there to die. Indeed Svay looked small and weak and his desire for death was still with him. It was nearly a miracle that he was still alive.

He told me one day, "Daran, I will die soon. I am not strong enough to survive. I have hidden some money and jewelry in the base of a palm tree near the rice field. After I die, I want you to go and take it."

I told him, "No, I will not take your money. What about your wife? Why don't you give those things to her?"

"I don't want to give anything to my wife. You know she hides when she has food to eat."

I said to him, "Bong," that is the Cambodian word for brother, "Bong, I cannot allow you to die. No one knows the future. If you eat and survive today, maybe tomorrow someone more powerful than the Khmer Rouge will take over our country and you will be saved. Maybe the Americans will come. Maybe the Red Cross will come. I will share my food with you and you can forget your unhappiness."

"No, Daran, you eat it. You don't have enough food yourself. I am old and tired."

After that I took him some of my oranges, but he wouldn't eat them. He only played music and kept his thoughts to himself. Before long he got sick. I went to Mr. Chhoeun and asked him to help me get some coconuts for Svay. At that time the Khmer Rouge counted coconuts every day to see if any were missing. Nevertheless, I stole two coconuts. Mr. Chhoeun agreed to help me. He took his hunting dogs away so they wouldn't bark when I went near the coconut trees.

Before I climbed the tree I looked around everywhere. I was scared. Finally I climbed up and took two. Mr. Chhoeun had said to take only one, but I thought Svay needed more. I took them to Svay and gave him one. He drank the water from it and began to feel much better. The next day when the soldier came to count coconuts, he said the number was down two. He asked Mr. Chhoeun if he had seen anyone take them. Mr. Chhoeun told the soldier that they were rotten and had fallen.

"Where did they fall?" the soldier asked.

"They fell beneath the tree, but my dog dragged them off in the forest."

Svay was better for a while. Then as each day passed he became more depressed. At the quarry he hammered the rock but with hardly enough force to kill an insect. I went to him.

"Svay, please try. The soldiers will hit you with their sticks if you don't work. Come over here." I took Svay behind a huge rock. I cut down the branch of a tree to use for loosening the rock with leverage. "See, brother, do it like this," I told him. We stood behind the rock so the soldiers couldn't see us.

"Svay, please! I don't want you to die. I want you to teach me how to write music. I don't know how to write music." He agreed to teach me, but still he stood there without working. I rocked my body back and forth and held his arm so he would rock with me and it would look like we were working. Together we rocked and talked softly.

Svay said, "Daran, my body is ready to die. But when my body disappears, my voice will remain. This is my voice. Listen to this voice say, 'I have seen your actions. I have seen your compassion for our people. That is good. Your goodness will save you.'"

I began to cry. "Oh, Svay," I said. "Someday I will compose a song about you because you have aimed me for the future, just as my father did."

I left Svay there behind the rock. I never saw him again, nor did anyone else. But each time I played music I thought about him. And I thought, too, of all the musicians and artists of Cambodia. Indeed Cambodia is a land of artists bound by a common love of creation. We are called to dance, to paint, to carve, to weave, to compose, to design. We build temples with an instinct like birds building nests. Artists had always been held in high esteem in Cambodian life. I thought of the dancers—three hundred royal dancers dancing by candlelight six hundred years before. Along with music, dances were part of the rites of passage. Each dance is connected to a myth, a ritual, or a historic event. The most famous dancers were the beautiful Apsara. They are carved everywhere in Angkor Wat, flying above kings and demons, above all the common people and creatures of the forest. Their three-pronged elaborate headdresses characterize their celestial spirit. The dancers use slow, graceful hand, finger, and foot movements accentuated by carved arm and ankle bracelets. There is no improvisation. The four thousand five hundred dance movements were the same in 1978 as they were five hundred years before. To dance was to feel the collective spirit of the Cambodian people in our bones.

I heard Svay's voice telling me to release my spirit—to bring comfort to the suffering. And so I did. Playing his compositions resurrected his soul and the spirits of all the musicians and artists of Cambodia killed by the Khmer Rouge. It was as if they joined me in a performance and all together we had such power and strength it seemed it could even penetrate the rock of the quarry.

Svay died in August or September 1978. Alone I sat with the memory of the death of Svay and my Chamroeun. All that solitude and sorrow made me weak and I came down with another case of malaria. It was so bad I began to have convulsions and again I was sent to the village to recover. When I got some of my strength back, the soldiers told me I would not be returned to the cooperative. Instead I would be given another assignment: grave digger.

At that time I was living in a small house near the graveyard. It was a terrible time for me. The graves were not very deep and sometimes animals would dig up the bodies and tear them to pieces. There was a constant stench in the air and the insistent sound of buzzing flies. Each time someone died, I went to collect their body and was given their ration of food for the day. And though it was hardly more than water and a few grains of rice, it gave me added strength—a kind of strength that came like a gift from the dead. The children I could carry in my arms. The adults I laid on a coconut frond and dragged. As I dug the graves, I remembered years before, watching my mother planting vegetables and flowers. After a time, the flowers grew up from the earth, fragrant and beautiful. But when I put the bodies in the ground, the earth just swallowed them and they disappeared.

Many people would be afraid of living in a graveyard. I wasn't afraid. After the Khmer Rouge, I wasn't afraid of ghosts or tigers or anything. The people buried in the graveyard were people I knew. I knew their faces, I knew their names. There was a baby on the right. A man with a face like so was buried here and a woman with beautiful hands there. I had laid their bodies in the graves myself. I put them in the ground to sleep. I wasn't afraid.

I played my accordion often then. I played music for all the people preparing to die and all the people not ready to die. I played a special song during that time, a lullaby sung by all Cambodian mothers. It's not a song anyone composed. Each mother chooses the words herself for her child alone. I used to play to make everyone, living and dead, sleep in peace and forget their unhappiness. I played that song and imagined all the people rising out of their graves and surrounding me to listen to their mothers' voices, to forget, and to sleep in peace. Whenever I play that song, I return to that time and place.

As the days and weeks and months passed, the circumstances of my life became more desperate. I began to eat rats. I ate anything that would let me survive a few days more.

After so many years of living as I had with so little food and so much death, I exhausted myself. I cannot say I gave up hope. I felt no hope. I felt nothing at all. I was empty. My body was so thin and light and numb it did not seem to belong to me. I began to think about my father all the time. I felt him standing beside me. I could hear his voice, but I couldn't see him. I wished I had some souvenir to remember him, but all I had were my memories—my memories and my bones.

Then I began to think perhaps my father had given me something, something invisible, but more powerful than things seen. My father had told me I was the representative of our family. I believed him, and I survived one more day.

Now I am nearing the end of my story and a memory that still pervades my soul. During the four years the Khmer Rouge ruled Cambodia, there were many purges. The older Khmer Rouge soldiers were constantly being replaced by younger ones. The older ones were sent to other areas of the country or killed for suspected disloyalty or for making mistakes.

In late 1978, one of the leaders, Mr. Prang, told me a new group of leaders was coming to our cooperative, and they were planning to kill me. He told me, "Daran, it is your turn. You must run away." I don't know why he told me. Maybe he felt he was a victim of the Khmer Rouge too. But how could I run away? The threat of death flooded me with fear, of course, but the soldiers would shoot me if I fled. Even if they did not, where would I go and how could I survive? I did not have the strength to live in the forest again. I could only sit in my house and cry and pray that I would not die.

To comfort myself I played a song on my accordion. It was a piece I used to play to accompany my mother's singing. Playing it made me feel, once again, my mother's soft touch on my head as she stroked my hair. I sat in the doorway of my house and played my accordion all evening and into the night. I did not stop to eat. I felt no hunger. I felt nothing. I watched the moonlight moving around the room, the shadows coming and going.

The man who lived across the road heard my playing. He came to my window and whispered, "Don't play so loud. And please don't play those songs of the republic. The soldiers will get irritated with you. Please, Daran, it's too dangerous. It is so bad in Cambodia now."

I told him, "No, tonight I must play."

He looked at me with a sad face and said, "No, Daran. If you play, you will die tonight. These will be your last hours."

His words meant nothing. I could not stop playing. I don't know why. To the people sleeping in their graves I said, "This is the last time you will hear the accordion's voice. Soon I will join you. I am waiting for death now."

The music invited my mind to drift and I returned to my childhood—back to summer holidays and the time of the Unity Celebration. There were two boatloads of children sailing on the Tonle Sap: a boat of boys sailing west, the girls sailing east. Then the boats began to approach each other. When they were close enough for the eyes of the boys and the eyes of the girls to meet, each group splashed so much water into the boat of the other that at last the boats sank and the children were thrown in the lake with gales of laughter. There were screams, too, from those who could not swim. But no one was allowed to drown, for that was a time of renewal and confirmation of life. It was a special time when the Mekong rose and backed up into the lake. The river's waters actually flowed backwards, and the lake became so full that it extended itself into the forest. It was there that the fish gave birth to their young. In this celebration of life, the drowning children were saved and the boys and girls paired up and swam off together to the shore where they feasted on the fruit of the forest and young love.

Meanwhile I continued to play as the moon rose bigger and brighter than I could ever recall. The sky was clear, reaching to eternity, and the night air was filled with my song. For hours I surrounded myself with the sound. I played every song that entered my mind, even the forbidden ones. I was a child again. I returned to my eighth year when Chamroeun taught me how to play the accordion. He was sitting behind me. I was nestled in his legs and his hands and fingers were over mine. We played together and he sang in my ear the old songs of Cambodia, love songs, French songs, songs to make people dance. We played funny songs that made us tumble over in laughter and lullabies a mother sings to quiet her babies and put them to sleep. That night I played them all again and talked to Chamroeun and felt peace.

As the night grew darker, I heard a bird cry out like someone in agony. I heard a dog howl. I softened the voice of my accordion and listened. I heard footsteps. I heard the sound of chickens rustling in their cages. I heard footsteps growing closer. I knew I was going to die. But I kept playing my accordion while thinking of my mother and father. I played a song about respecting the spirit of one's parents.

The sound of the soldiers' footsteps grew closer, then stopped. They were listening to me. Were they thinking, remembering, feeling? Were they longing? Then they were in front of me in their black uniforms with their red scarves and guns. I knew it was too late. My music had revealed me.

Seeing me there with my accordion must have surprised them because they did not shoot. Despite all my years of struggle and survival, at this moment I felt I would die at the hands of these men. I looked at their faces and into their eyes. Though my music had saved me many times in the preceding years, the icy cruelty of these men terrified me and I thought nothing could save me. I played to the end of my song. My heart beat frantically. I began to shake.

The soldiers looked at each other and one of them ordered me to play. But I was so frightened and shook so much, I could not. He hit me with his gun and said, "Play or I will kill you!" So I started to play a song, but it did not please them. Another soldier hit me on the back of my neck and told me to play a particular song of the Communist Party. But how could I play a song I had never heard? The soldiers waited, growing impatient, while I looked out the window to the sky and prayed to my mother and father, begging them to help me.

Then suddenly, without thought, without intention, without will, I started to play the song the soldiers wanted. I played beautifully, fluidly, like someone else was guiding my fingers. I felt the undeniable presence of my brother Chamroeun. The soldiers were pleased at the sound. They smiled and laid down their guns. They sat down surrounding me in a circle. I was surprised but greatly relieved. Huge tears fell from my eyes and splashed on my hands and on my accordion. My pounding heart quieted.

As my fear was replaced by calm, anger began to well up in me—an anger unlike anything I had ever experienced. I hated these men intensely. I hated them with every drop of blood, energy, and life within me. I hated them for what they had done to Cambodia. I hated them for their brutality against my parents, against my only sister, against my beloved brothers who looked like me. In my mind I could see my father buried in the ground with only his bloodied head showing. I saw my gentle mother raped and shot. I saw my youngest brother, Rithy, the boy always in motion, swung by the legs against sharp rocks until his six-year-old body lay dead. I saw my childhood home dismantled and empty. I saw my forest companions dead and alone. I saw my friend Svay and all my beautiful Cambodian people thin, broken, and lifeless. I hated these men for their lack of mercy, their callousness, their selfishness. They were beasts!

The soldiers sat with their eyes closed. They were weaponless and vulnerable. I wanted to jump up, take their guns, and shoot them. The opportunity lay before me like an invitation. But for reasons I do not understand, I did nothing.

Then, out of the sky or out of my body or out of my accordion, I do not know from where, came the voices of my parents. They said: "Do not move. Only sit and play your music. Play it, our young sweet son. Play it with all your strength. Play it with all the love we have given you. Play it with all the forgiveness we have taught you. Play it with all the mercy others have offered you. Play it until you cannot play it anymore." I listened to their voices and my anger subsided with every breath I exhaled.

I continued to play as if I were someplace where fear did not exist. After a time the soldiers grew sleepy, gathered up their guns, and left without saying anything more. For a few moments I believed I had once more been saved from death. I began to play my accordion again. Suddenly I wanted to play "Svay Chante," the song that had come to me when I was only a child and saw the accordion for the first time on the day the musicians came to play at the temple of Ang Chan. I wanted to hear its words of yearning for love.

After a few minutes, one of the soldiers returned. He came close to me and said, "I've been ordered to kill you."

I looked up at him. He was a young man but he looked old. His eyebrows pointed downward around his eyes. He had a scar on his right cheek, and the red cloth of the executioner was tied around his wrist. I stared at the pulse rising and falling in his neck. I ignored what he had said.

I began to play my accordion. If I was going to die, I wanted to die playing my accordion. The music took me back in my mind to where I began this story: with the song "Svay Chante." The music surrounded me like incense rising in a ceremony of remembrance. In my mind was my father's voice, Chamroeun's fingers, my accordion surrounded by candles. I played and thought of the old man asking if I could tear open the chest. At that moment I felt I was tearing open my chest, making myself vulnerable and exposed like Ang Chan at the temple near my home. I bent down as Prince Sihanouk, in my dream, had not. I gave up and I bent down as if this soldier who had come to kill me was a god. I felt the collective spirit of the Cambodian people. I felt the presence of the king-master and the angels. And I was no longer angry or afraid. I played that song with all the joy I had ever felt.

The soldier did not shoot me. He listened until the end of the song. Then he said in a small, quiet voice, "Will you teach me to play?"

"Yes," I said. Yes was all I had left to say.

The soldier laid down his gun and sat beside me. His hands were trembling so badly I helped him touch the keys. We played for a while and agreed to meet again.

He got up to go. Then the most extraordinary thing happened. This man looked deep into my eyes and must have seen himself reflected there because he said: "I am a Khmer Rouge soldier. I am trained to kill my own parents if ordered to. So why can't I kill you? What stops me from killing you?"

I did not answer because I did not know. We looked at each other in silence and the distance between us disappeared. The soldier then turned and left. When I was alone I cried and sat for a long while watching the flickering flame of my torch. "I am sorry," I said to the air. "I am sorry, Mother and Father, I did not die and join you. I will join you someday, but for now I have been given life and I must take

it. I must take it for myself and for the others I might help."
I blew out the flame. The morning light then streamed
through the window. It was the beginning of a new day.

I did not know it at the time, but the Khmer Rouge regime
was falling apart. In addition to the failed regime's agricultural policies, Cambodia's relations with Vietnam were wors-
ening. In 1975, the Vietnamese tried to capture several islands
in the Gulf of Siam and after that Pol Pot did not trust them.
The Vietnamese communists patronized Cambodians and
believed that our revolution was of less importance than their
own. After Pol Pot strengthened his ties with China, Vietnam
reacted by signing a twenty-five-year treaty with the Soviet
Union. In 1977, Vietnam signed another treaty of coopera-
tion with Laos. Pol Pot saw this as further evidence of the
conspiracy against his regime. He spoke of an illness in the
Communist Party caused by "evil microbes."

Pol Pot believed that the Cambodians living in the south-
ern part of Vietnam would rise up and overthrow the Vietnamese. When this did not happen, he suspected treason and
allowed a merciless massacre. He rounded up the military
officers in charge of the area and sent them to Tuol Sleng,
where, after their confessions, they were photographed and
executed.

By early December 1978, the Vietnamese held several roads
around Phnom Penh. By the end of the month, one hundred
thousand Vietnamese troops began a major offensive on the
northeastern border of Cambodia. On January 7, 1979, Pol
Pot escaped Phnom Penh by helicopter to seek refuge in
China, leaving behind three million dead and four million
starving people.

The people knew nothing of this in the cooperatives. We
continued to survive day by day. The day after my encounter
with the soldiers, I hunted for food. I caught three rabbits

and took them to the house of the section leader. As I approached the house, I heard an American radio broadcast. The announcer said the Vietnamese had invaded Cambodia to overthrow the Khmer Rouge. I took a deep breath. I waited a few minutes and then entered the house to give the rabbits to Angkar. The section leader turned off his radio and quickly dismissed me. I went to the others and told them what I had heard. No one believed me at first. I said, "Believe me. Trust me. I heard it with my own ears."

As the day wore on, we heard bombs exploding. The sound grew closer and closer and we all grew tense. The Khmer Rouge told us it was just the explosives loosening rock at the mine, but we noticed they were nervous, and we watched the leaders hurry to hold a meeting among themselves. Others began to think that the radio broadcast had been true.

At about eight o'clock that night, the leaders rounded up all the people of the cooperative and told us, "Go now!"

"Go where?" we asked.

"Go home! Go home!"

We looked at each other and repeated the words. Gradually the words sank into our ears and we walked away hugging each other. We hardly had any energy, but we danced and sang songs we thought we had forgotten.

It was utterly dark that night. The moon had gone somewhere. We walked away in every direction. We had become so disoriented by starvation and terror we hardly knew which way to go. I took my accordion and walked in the direction of my home village. Though there was no path, I followed my instinct like a fish returning to the place of its birth. Other people walked in other directions. Some went the wrong way and fell into a crevasse and I heard their voices as they fell. I was afraid of falling, too, but I put my hand out in front of me and just kept walking. I walked until I heard the voice of a train and I followed the sound. Finally, the morning light came and I saw railroad tracks and then I knew how to get back home, back to my farm, back to the river, back to the temple.

I walked along the tracks in a worn black shirt which barely covered my thin, scarred body. I loosened it from my body and it blew off in the wind. I was free. I allowed the sunlight to soak into my skin.

A train went by full of Khmer Rouge soldiers escaping the invading Vietnamese. People who couldn't fit inside were hanging onto the outside. One of these people was a man without legs who fell from the train. This man called for me to bring him some water. We were near a log bridge over a dried-up river. I went down the bank and dug in the ground until I found some water. I put some in my hands and ran up the bank to give it to the man. When I reached him there was only a bit left. I did this several times until he felt better.

In a quiet voice the man asked me to take off his shirt. I saw he had been shot in the chest. He put my hands over the hole so he could talk. He said, "I am a Mulatan. I've fought for Angkar. You can see I lost my legs because of war. And I killed my mother myself. My own mother. I hate Angkar now!" He began to cry.

The man was dying and his voice lowered to a whisper. He pronounced his words slowly, one by one. "My brother's name is Mao. Bury me and tell Mao where he can find my bones. Put some words on my grave. Say not to go to war. And carve my name. My name is Moeun."

I buried Moeun in the place where I had taken the water. And then I stopped thinking about death. I only looked straight ahead and played my accordion—the accordion that had been a gift from my enemy. I thought of how that accordion had been my companion and my savior, how music had awakened me and led me to fruit, how I had found an accordion on the stump of a tree. I thought of the music and the firelight keeping at bay the darkness of death, the pit of rotting bodies, the serpents, the hordes of demons, the starvation and despair. And I thought of how I always had songs to stir memories of those I loved and those who loved me.

The accordion had a hole in it and made a strange sound, but I played a song I composed myself. Its sound gave me a peace I had not felt since I was a small child in my father's arms in a Cambodia without war. That accordion sang to me with a raspy old human voice, a voice wounded but alive. It was alive with a spirit that followed me through many more difficult years, across the ocean, and to this day here with you.

This is my story. It is not merely true, but deeply true, and now you must know me to my bones. I did not know this story would be so long. But since you asked, I remembered, and I answered.

Reprise

And so my first question to Daran—how did you survive—
was not an easy question to answer. He said it was love and
music and invisible hands that saved him. Perhaps too it was
because through those long years of suffering, his father's
voice kept reminding him that he was the representative of
his family. Daran felt responsible for keeping the flame of life
alive. It shone through him like light reflected in a mirror,
because even his enemies saw the sacredness of life in him
and even they, in all their brutality, could not kill it.

Daran lived under the Vietnamese-installed government in
Cambodia until 1984 when he escaped into Thailand. In
1988, after four years in a refugee camp, he was admitted to
the United States as a humanitarian parolee. He now makes
his living as a social worker, gardens, and revives his memories with the accordion.

Pol Pot, Ieng Sary, Khieu Samphan, and the other leaders
of the Khmer Rouge have never been tried for the estimated
three million deaths that occurred during their reign.

Bree Lafreniere grew up in a small town in Oregon and was introduced to the outside world by way of missionaries returned from Africa. After earning a B.A. in sociology from the University of Oregon, she served as a Peace Corps volunteer in the Solomon Islands where she began writing. Bree has worked with refugees since 1989. She lives in Tacoma, Washington, with her two daughters, Isabella and Sophia.

Daran Kravanh was born in Kampong Chhnang province, Cambodia, and arrived in the United States as a refugee in 1988. In 1996 he received a B.A. from Evergreen State College. He was the Student of the Year for Tacoma Community College in 1992. In 1997 he was awarded a Humanitarian Award from the city of Tacoma and currently serves on the Human Rights Commission for the city. Daran is active in Cambodian cultural life and works for the state of Washington. He has two sons, Kiry and Chunneath.